NINE LIVES:
A Self-Help Book
for Amputees

By Ian Colquhoun

ISBN: 978-1-291-41932-0

www.publishnation.co.uk

About the Author

Ian Colquhoun is an actor, author and folk music promoter from Livingston in Scotland but who now resides in Edinburgh. He studied history at Edinburgh University from 2004 and has been in a multitude of films and TV shows since losing his legs in an arson attack in 2002. Up until then he had worked as a warehouseman. He supports Hibernian FC and his keenest areas of interest are the Jacobite Wars in Scotland and Ireland, and the various colonial conflicts of the 19th century.
www.iancolquhoun.org.uk

This particular book was first published by the now defunct Piper's Ash Publishing in 2008. Consequently, it was written before the Tory-led Coalition's persecution of the sick and disabled began. This is a re-release. 50% of all profits will be donated to amputee charities.

Acknowledgements

I would like to thank the following people for all of their help, encouragement and inspiration over the last few years, and for helping to make this book possible.

Firstly, Susie and Marjorie at the Murray foundation.

Nicola and Paige Allan.
Keith Ferguson.
Joe McGuire
Ian and Johan Graham
Louise Mitchell
Kelly Cumming
Colin Duthie
Richard Vallis

My family, David ' Disco' McDermott, Jenny Hood, Tony ' mad-dog' Divers, Robert Hogg, Mikey Williamson, Samantha McAfferty, David Whynne, Chris Brown PhD, Sharon Adams MA, Stuart McHardy MA, Shug and everyone at the Commie, Steve Richards, Alana Herron, Richard Madely, Judy Finnigan, Sean Patey, Hibeesbounce, Lynn Nelson, Lynn Davidson, Sandra Dick, everyone from Craigshill, Olivia Giles, Mixu Paatelainen

Prelude

As an amputee myself, I found myself wanting to write a book like this, not only for artistic purposes, but also to have real stories about real people who have endured limb loss/absence readily available to anyone who needs them, be it for research purposes, information purposes or just for a good, interesting read. It may seem odd that I myself as the author am featured briefly, but this is because I was asked to feature myself by the other volunteers you will read about, and because one of my other volunteers pulled out at the last minute. I agreed with this suggestion as it makes sense, though I did have to get someone else to interview me in the exact same way that I interviewed the other volunteers.

I hope you enjoy reading this book.

KEITH FERGUSON : WALK TALL. STAND TALL

"FIGHT AS HARD AS YOU CAN. DON'T REFUSE HELP. KEEP YOUR SENSE OF HUMOUR."

Driving along the M8 motorway listening to dance music. Not just any old dance music, but Ibiza style dance music. Classic Euphoria. Following his football team across Europe and going on trips to the World Cup and Euro competitions with his friend Alan. Sounds like the activities that any young man in his late teens or early twenties might indulge in on a regular basis, don't they? Keith Ferguson is no whippersnapper though, but he is by no means an old man either.

Keith was born in 1952. Into a very different society with very differing attitudes to a multitude of issues. Keith has been an amputee since he was only two years old.

Keith was born with *congenital birth abnormalities* that resulted in his left leg being amputated very high above his left knee, just below the hip, when he was two years old. Drastic life changing surgery at an early age. That in itself, particularly in those days, was a monumental amputation to have. But it didn't stop there. Keith's remaining leg, his right, also gave him a multitude of problems as a child as it wouldn't develop properly at the same rate as the rest of his body. It wasn't growing. Keith suffered a lot of pain because of this. Numerous operations and procedures were tried, but all to no avail. This really started to affect Keith more when he became a young teenager and then a young man, as the problems with his right leg meant that he was only five foot and one inch tall in height.

Keith now jokes, "It was getting as if I would be able to drag my knuckles along the ground."

Though thankfully it wasn't that bad, it was nevertheless not so good for a man's self esteem, especially when you're already wearing a wooden leg with an above knee amputation.

Having had the amputation at two years old, Keith was issued with a wooden prosthetic leg when the time was right. His first school was Gorgie Special School, which was a school not only for the physically disabled, but for the mentally disabled as well. That in itself shows how little people, and in particular the authorities at the time, understood all aspects of disability. His main memory of that school, asides the hazard of fellow pupils trying to set his wooden leg on fire on occasion, was the school nativity play when he was seven. Keith played one of the shepherds.

"All of Edinburgh's council and education bigwigs were there, including the city's Lord Provost, and the play was going well until the angel came down to deliver the message to the shepherds."

One of the other two shepherds, both of whom were classed as "nutcases" in those days on account of their mental problems, took a fit and started attacking the realistic flock of toy sheep at the front of the stage, one of which he launched directly at the city's Lord Provost. The child then launched into a foul mouthed tirade that embarrassed everyone present, and saw the poor unfortunate child carted off stage leaving the play to continue with just two shepherds.

Keith's only other significant memory of his time at the 'special' school was when one day he was photographed alongside a female fellow pupil in a Wendy House, alongside a man in a suit. He, of course, thought nothing of it at the time.

Shortly afterwards in the run up to an election, pamphlets were put through everyone in the local area's door showing this photograph, pamphlets that claimed that the Conservative Party candidate in the photograph spent a lot of his spare time working with under privileged and disabled kids, which of course was a pack of lies.

The candidate had shamefully used Keith and the girl to his own ends, a practice that, thankfully, no one would get away with nowadays.

"I had an auntie who at the time was very active in the Labour Party and was in attendance at a meeting where questions could be asked of rival candidates."

When the Conservative candidate claimed to have visited the school on a number of occasions, Keith's auntie exposed him as being a barefaced liar, as he had only attended the school once on a fleeting visit to get the photograph taken.

"She didn't get to say much else though; she was dragged out of the meeting for unmasking this liar with her outburst. No wonder I've been into socialism since!"

Eventually Keith's mum decided that particular school was no good for her son and decided to have him sent to a mainstream school. The council were at first belligerent, insisting that he attend the 'special' school, but they eventually relented and told Keith's parents that if they could find a 'normal' school to take him, then that would be fine.

"My mum went to see the headmistress of Stenhouse Primary School and she was fine about me going there".

Keith encountered little or no taunting or problems at primary school, though the folly of the lack of disability awareness in society was shown when everyone in his class was asked to write a story.

"We were asked to write our name at the top of it. I was pulled up by my teacher for only writing 'Keith' on the top of my piece of paper. My teacher wanted me to write my surname too, but because I had been sent to the 'special' school I was behind and didn't know how to write my surname yet."

Thankfully his teacher was very understanding, and within a few months Keith caught up.

Though struggling along with a very basic artificial leg, Keith found his condition did have some small advantages.

"I didn't have to stand in line in the playground and I got to skip the queue for school dinners so that I wasn't standing up for too long. I even got to use a different exit from the school that involved less of a walk to get home, and I was allowed two friends to go with me on this route. I soon had them all on a kind of rota system for escaping via this handy exit, and this helped me make new friends".

On his first day at secondary school at the Royal High in Edinburgh on Regent Road, Keith experienced an embarrassing moment on account of a teacher's insensitivity.

"We were all in the school hall, which had steep rows of seats at the side making it like a kind of amphitheatre, but while the teacher was talking to the other kids I was allowed to sit right up the back so I didn't have to tackle the stairs".

This teacher then embarrassed Keith by getting the other one hundred and twenty new pupils to turn around and stare at him, whilst the teacher told them that this was the "new boy called Keith with the bad leg, and that they were all to be nice to him and try not to knock him over".

Keith found this very patronising, and was also a little daunted by all the staring in his direction.

"It was ironic too; within a week that same teacher gave me a row for 'skipping' the dinner queue."

Thankfully, disability awareness is much better these days.

Keith had to repeat second year at high school as he had to have a year off while doctors and surgeons tried painstaking and drastic limb lengthening procedures on his remaining right leg. The periods of waiting in between these procedures were frustrating, as it was a question of waiting on the bone to re-grow into where the limb had been lengthened. Eventually they managed to add about two inches to Keith's leg, but the next stage of the treatment and its subsequent operation were to be carried out at the start of the summer holidays. It got worse. Just before he was about to be taken in for the operation, Keith was told that the first long drawn out stage of treatment hadn't worked. It would have to be done again. Eventually he got his operation and found out something rather surprising about himself.

"I've never been a violent man, but anaesthetic makes me violent and aggressive when I start to come round, they had to strap me to my bed and nervously check to see if I was fully awake before they undid the straps."

To this day there is a warning in Keith's notes that he may behave aggressively after anaesthetic, but that is by no means rare. It's a common phenomenon.

Even after all this though, there were still serious problems with his right leg. Another solution doctors tried was taking a 'wedge' out of his knee, but that didn't work either, making him kind of go knock kneed on that side, and the procedure even made him lose what little extra height he had gained.

During his time in hospital Keith found that ignorance regarding disability could be found in the most seemingly unlikely places. While he was on a 'boys only' ward, a priest would visit the boys and come and ask each boy how he was and generally see if they were ok. It was a different story when one Church of Scotland minister did his rounds on the same ward. For one thing, before engaging any of these ill, frightened boys in conversation, he would check the clipboard at the end of their bed to see if they were COS. What really annoyed Keith though was, understandably, the minister's reaction.

Keith told the minister "Well I'm in a lot of pain, it's really bad".
The minister coldly declared that this must be God's will.

"I thought, you what? This is God's will?"

An understandably infuriated and upset Keith then answered the minister, in such a way that that he never came back to visit him again. Ignorance of disability was commonplace in all walks of life back then though, again, attitudes are improving today.

Having finally went back to re-sit second year, Keith found school quite heavy going after such a long absence and illness. "It was very demanding physically."

One bright spot about going to school was that due to his disability, Keith was entitled to have a car take him to school, provided by the Edinburgh Corporation, the old equivalent of the city council. He was flabbergasted to find out on the first day he got such a lift to school, that not only was he being picked up by a chauffeur, the chauffeur was driving a massive Daimler.

"The corporation had about six or seven cars at the time, things like Daimlers and big Mercedes that they normally used for the Lord Provost or when the city had a visiting dignitary like the Queen or a foreign diplomat. Whatever car was spare was usually sent to pick me up. Though I was sent a taxi sometimes, when all the Corporation's cars were otherwise engaged. The kids in my own year at school knew why I arrived in such a car but some of the other kids assumed I was a millionaire or something."

By the age of eighteen, Keith admits that the pressures of growing up, his disability and his lack of height had made him a tad disillusioned and embittered with it all.

"I ignored the advice of my school by opting to move to London and get a job rather than going to university. I got a flat near Brisbane Road, home of Leyton Orient FC, and I got a job in an office with Lloyds Bank."

By this time Keith's leg was a little better and as he had a job and a 'season ticket' for the London underground, he carefully scanned the papers every week to see what teams were playing in London.

"I got to see a lot of Chelsea, as well as a multitude of other teams. I had the privilege of seeing Bobby Charlton and the late great George Best playing for Manchester United, and I even used my half day "Christmas shopping holiday" from work to fulfil a lifetime's ambition, visiting Anfield and seeing the Kop, while Tottenham Hotspur took on Liverpool in the League Cup."

You may have gathered from this chapter that Keith is a bit of a football fan.

Keith wasn't the first Scot to head south to London in search of a new life, or at least a break from life in Scotland itself, nor was he the last, but to do so with one artificial limb and having had so many problems on the other leg took enormous courage and determination. He shared a flat with a couple of guys down there and lived a bit of the high life, sometimes literally, experimenting with LSD and cannabis, as a lot of people were in those days.

"I found those drugs I experimented with a little boring."

He still worked though, still walked, and he had the football to look forward to, coming home to Edinburgh on the weeks Hearts were playing at home, and watching an English side of his choice on the other weeks. He was even at the famous Arsenal v Newcastle tie when the infamous Jimmy Hill was forced to take over as a linesman.

Keith's stay in London ended when he came home to Edinburgh after his dad had suffered a major heart attack, requiring him to stay off work for at least six months. Keith moved back home and got a job with the Bank of Scotland, doing similar work to what he had been doing in London. Then he switched careers and got a job as an export clerk at Edinburgh Airport. He has worked in the distribution and export business ever since.

Despite his successful career switch, by the age of twenty two Keith was getting depressed. He had a few girlfriends but his self consciousness about his height and his amputation affected his relationships and got him down. Things came to a head when he met with a surgeon called Mr Lamb at the now defunct Princess Margaret Rose Hospital in Edinburgh.

7

"I didn't even mean it to happen, I just broke down and told him I couldn't take the pain or the height thing any more, I had had enough."

Mr Lamb offered Keith a solution. Keith and his doctor decided that given all the problems he was having with pain, and the way his reduced height was affecting his self confidence, the best solution was to have the 'bad' foot amputated. It was decided that Keith would be best having what is known as a Syme's amputation, where the foot is amputated but the heel is retained and padded out with a flap of skin. It sounds like a drastic procedure but, although he spent three months in hospital, there were to be some very positive outcomes for Keith.

Firstly, the operation eradicated a lot of his pain, though he still needed some morphine from time to time immediately after the procedure. Secondly, and perhaps crucially, because his foot was amputated, doctors were able to add another seven inches onto Keith's height.

"I couldn't believe it, I went into hospital five foot one and came out of hospital five foot eight." He was in hospital for three months this time, all in.

The change in his height given to Keith by the Syme's operation changed his life drastically and for the better.

"I was now able to look people in the eye or even look down on people who had previously been taller than me. It was an enormous boost, literally."

The only immediate drawback for Keith was adapting to going for a pee again as his new height meant he had to learn to re adjust his aim, as it were.

"When you've been used to peeing from a certain height for so long you have to learn to readjust your trajectory a little, and it can take a bit of getting used to."

Keith, of course, soon adapted to that and admits it was a miniscule drawback in comparison to the benefits his operation and new height afforded him. Keith had initially asked to be made even taller than five foot eight but the doctor said no - "I probably would have fallen over" joked Keith.

Keith's Syme's amputated side was fitted with a limb soon after the procedure and he was allowed to go home from hospital on the condition that he came back in every three days to have his leg checked by the sister.

"She thought I was walking about too much when I was on the ward, but I think she just wanted to check if I was over- doing things too soon. She did warn me sensibly that if my wound showed any signs of redness I would be readmitted to the ward straight away."

Things changed for Keith forever during his spell on the ward. His new height meant he needed new clothes like trousers and he wanted a long overcoat. He also needed to change shoe size and was advised to 'up' from a size five to a size nine. He told a gorgeous nurse on the ward called Anne that he had saved up money and would be going shopping soon. She enquired as to whether Keith was going shopping on his own and offered to go with him. The shopping trip turned into a drink afterwards and the two eventually saw each other for about six months. Keith went into hospital for a make or break operation, the gamble paid off, and he even pulled a gorgeous nurse! Hollywood itself couldn't have scripted it better. All thanks to his elective amputation and the burst of confidence he got from his new height.

.

After that operation Keith's life really took off. He rose through the ranks of his company and has since worked all over the world for three big companies, including Sun Microsystems and Dutch distribution company Frans Maas. Keith got engaged to a girl named Patricia when he was twenty four but that didn't work out, but although he was upset about that at the time, he soon bounced back. He made up for a lot of lost time between the age of twenty two and when he met and married his lovely wife Grace in 1979, when he was thirty.

Keith joked "the number one song in the chart at the time was 'we don't talk anymore' by Cliff Richard, if that's not a good omen I don't know what is."

Keith is another amputee who, in many respects, has never lost his sense of humour.

Then in the mid nineties things started to go a little wrong again.

"There were pressures. I'm a born worrier anyway but the stress of having a young family, having to work twice as hard as everyone else to prove a point and the physical exertion of walking so much, coupled with all the travelling and involvement with the local amateur football setup took their toll on me. I started to get depressed."

His Doctor and some later tests confirmed that he was indeed severely depressed, due to Serotonin depletion, the chemical in the brain that makes us happy.

"No one believed me when I eventually told them I was depressed, they were shocked, particularly as I was usually the one who was laughing and joking and had a good job etc. Perhaps my personality and my job masked that a bit."

In layman's terms, Keith reckons his depression was caused by burnout, pure and simple. All the ups and down of the previous years finally catching up with him. Perfectly understandable, and people often get depressed over far less trivial things in life than Keith has encountered. He deserves great credit.

"I was put on medication and although I was still down for a while, after about six months I felt like a new man. I felt better than I had done in fifteen years."

Keith's work life hasn't been without its ups and downs. A sicko new colleague started work with Keith and there were disputes and fallings out, and although Keith received an apology from the chairman of the company, that chairman left soon after. Keith's new boss, the sicko, then clearly had it in for him. Keith was put under a lot of unnecessary pressure and eventually ended up on Garden Leave, awaiting redundancy, because of this ambitious cretin who wanted to make a name for himself. Keith's not stupid though, and got himself some good representation that ultimately got him a good honest settlement from his old employer, with a sweet sting in the tail. Soon after he signed a compromise agreement, he was offered a job that involved auditing, and checking the work of the man who had previously hounded him out of his old job. Keith was the bigger man though and pursued no personal vendetta against the aforementioned individual once he got his new job.

Having won not only his battle to beat adversity in the workplace and battle his disability, Keith decided to become semi- retired in 2004. He took his sons to see Hearts' three away fixtures in the UEFA cup, which included trips to Portugal, Holland and Switzerland, though ultimately Hearts failed to qualify from the tough group they were drawn in. He now works for a company in Livingston and has been a volunteer hospital visitor for the Murray Foundation, making valuable trips to see new amputees in hospital, since 2007. He has also just started an advocacy pilot scheme for amputees, in conjunction with the Murray Foundation, to help them with all sorts of things like benefits, claims and workplace disputes. In this capacity he is not a mediator, he represents the amputee personally and uncompromisingly, to his great credit. He is glad to be out of life's "rat race."

"I get more of a thrill and sense of satisfaction from helping others than I ever did from my jobs, though I was good at them too."

Fitness wise, Keith used to enjoy swimming but doesn't go as often now, as the sessions set aside for disabled swimmers are usually at unsuitable times.

Keith gets minor phantom pains and sensations from time to time but describes them as "absolutely nothing compared to the pain I had before that last amputation".

He drives using *Jeff Gosling hand controls* and loves listening to Ibiza style trance and house whilst driving along, particularly after a successful advocacy or *amputee visiting* session. Thankfully he hasn't required any further amputations since he was twenty two, though that is a concern of his for the future, as it is with all amputees, as it may affect their mobility or stop them walking altogether, but for now, Keith's not unduly worried. Worrying about one's future mobility is common in all human beings, not just those who have lost limbs. Keith just wants to keep walking for as long as he can. He doesn't use a wheelchair at all, not even at home, which is amazing for a double lower limb amputee. He wears his limbs all day. On his right leg he wears a special Syme's prosthesis, his left above knee prosthesis has a *pneumatic knee* with a safety locking mechanism.

He doesn't drink a lot, though he enjoys the odd Bacardi and the odd session when Hearts win cups now and then. His favourite food is still good old egg and chips. He and Grace have three sons aged twenty two, twenty four and twenty. Keith has found that his own condition has made his kids more aware of disability, and that awareness has even rubbed off on some of their friends. One of the most inspiring moments in Keith's life was when he read a story one of his sons, Peter, had written at school, a story in which his son said how much he admired his dad and wanted to be just like him. "Tears were running down my face when I read it."

His highest point post- operation, when he was twenty two, was standing up at five foot eight, and going out with that nurse. His biggest personal inspiration has been his mother, particularly in his teenage years.

"A lot of my inspiration has come from within too; my doctor said I am a born fighter."

The only improvements Keith thinks the NHS needs regarding amputee care are more hospital visits from fellow amputees and perhaps a bit more help for patients when they are discharged, regarding benefits and things like that. Keith helps the NHS by giving voluntary lectures to physiotherapy students at Edinburgh's Queen Margaret University College.

GENERAL RATING OF NHS CARE – TEN OUT OF TEN.

Keith Ferguson and his life are both remarkable. Moving away to London is a big decision at the best of times, let alone when one is disabled. The decision to have his bad foot amputated proved to be one of the greatest decisions he has ever made. It is testament to Keith's fortitude and resilience that he is still a smiling warm approachable character who spends a great deal of his time helping others, while others who might be put in similar positions might just have curled up and given in.

He has battled limb loss, chronic pain, workplace harassment and discrimination, depression, broken romances and some tough decisions and came out of it all a strong, admirable man who does indeed stand tall. And walks proud. And he should do.

LOUISE MITCHELL: GETTING ON WITH IT

"Whatever life throws at you makes you stronger inside"

Mondays can be so tediously boring. Particularly if you work. In many cases the individual is either still recovering from whatever their excesses at the weekend may have been, or they have the sombre thought of another four days hard graft until it is the weekend again. It's fair to say that many people see completing their Monday shift as being a case of 'one down, four to go' , until the next weekend.

In March of 2005 one such person stepped of a train after work in West Lothian just like she always had done. It was Monday night. One down, four to go. She was on her way home. Until she was hit by a high speed train in an incident at the level crossing. This Monday, March 14th 2005, was to prove anything but humdrum for this young woman from East Calder. BANG. One minute you're on your way home from work, a few moments later your life has changed forever and you are fighting for your life.

Louise Calder Mitchell, who was twenty years old at the time, had up until then worked as a receptionist for a leading nationwide courier company, and had been living a life much like any of her peers would have been. Working during the week, going out drinking with various friends at the weekends, driving her car, and she had a particular interest in speedway , stock car racing and other boy racer type days that are held in various locations.

On that fateful Monday in March 2005, Louise was hit on a level crossing by a train that was doing about eighty miles per hour. The level crossing in question is notoriously dangerous and Louise is by no means the first person to be injured or killed on it.

"The train wasn't stopping in that particular station, it was an express train that was going right through, in some ways I was lucky because if it had been stopping in the station there is every chance I would have become trapped under it and dragged along further."

As it wasn't stopping, the train hit Louise like a battering ram and sent her flying through the air, causing the most horrific injuries. Brave Louise somehow remained conscious throughout all this, not even going into shock, but there was a shock in store for her when her despairing brother arrived at her side. Louise had lost her legs and one of her arms. She was now a treble amputee. But she was still alive!

"My brother told me that I had lost my arm and both of my legs. I remember it seemed to take the emergency services a long time to get to us. My brother was handed my arm as it was initially hoped that it could be re -attached to me, but the way in which it had came off meant that that was impossible. In a strange way though, the way my arm came off saved me as I might have bled to death had the *trauma injury* to it been different. My friend Marissa was there too. It wasn't until the emergency services arrived that I also realised I had a serious *degloved* back injury, the pain when they tried to move me was really bad from that."

A degloved injury is when an extensive portion of the skin is completely torn away from the tissue underneath, which is subsequently deprived of a blood supply. It is named by analogy to the process of removing a glove. Typically, degloving injuries affect the extremities and limbs; this is because any injury which would induce degloving of the head or torso is usually likely to be lethal. But thankfully, Louise's clothes were pulled up over the wound in her back to keep everything in and the result of that was that she survived the incident, for the time being. After being rushed to the local accident and emergency department, Louise spent eight days under sedation while doctors initially performed eight operations on her to *skin graft* what was left of her three damaged limbs, and also to try to rectify the gaping injury to her back.

"When I initially woke up from the sedation I was laughing, joking and hallucinating, common side effects of *morphine*. As they slowly reduced my dosage though I started to straighten up, though I still remember buzzing the nurses to tell them there was a wee boy about to fall off the hospital roof. The 'wee boy' was actually just a pipe on the wall that was visible from my hospital room window."

Though she had lost three limbs, the medical staff's main concern was the injury to Louise's back. Louise spent two months in St John's Hospital before being transferred to a rehabilitative hospital in Edinburgh, Astley Ainslie. It was planned that once there she would undergo rehabilitation and hopefully be fitted with prosthetic limbs. Walking would be a tough task though, Louise has her left leg amputated through the knee, the right leg just above the knee and her left arm amputated above the elbow, so not only would she have the increased difficulty of trying to walk with no knees, she might have problems getting upright as she now had only one hand with which

16

to lever herself up or use a crutch. Before Louise learned all that though, she would need physiotherapy and would need to be shown how to *transfer* and get used to her wheelchair. A tough task, but Louise was ready for it. This timetable was sadly thrown out of the window only four weeks after she was admitted to rehab though, when her back wound became infected and she was rushed back to *St John's*.

"My back was in a bit of a mess, the skin around the wound was infected and dying and I eventually caught *septicaemia* (blood poisoning). I really wasn't well. I thought I was going to die this time for sure. I thought I was a goner."

Louise underwent a further four operations on her back during this second spell in St John's, before being transferred back to Astley Ainslie to start her rehabilitation again.

Louise was discharged from Astley Ainslie after seven months without a set of prosthetic limbs, as there were still problems with her stumps, though she was cast and fitted with some, including one that had a Playboy logo *laminated into the socket*. She did get upright on that limb, but problems with her other leg have meant that the limb fitting process has been delayed, for the time being anyway.

"The biggest problem at the time for me regarding prosthetics was finding a suitable limb for my through knee amputated side, various systems were tried but weren't suitable, I was also having trouble getting myself upright so that I could get the leg to lock straight. I was glad to get out of hospital that October even without my limbs though, as I missed my friends and family and deep down, I knew that I needed to learn how to get on with things in the real world rather than being in hospital where everything is done for you. I wanted to get on with my life"

Being discharged from hospital without limbs must have been disheartening for Louise, though she was also no doubt glad to see the back of the place after being in for nine months too. Louise has became firm friends with a nurse named Lesley who works on the amputee rehabilitation ward, and the two regularly enjoy nights in and mad nights out together, as Louise still does with some of her other friends.

"My wheelchair doesn't stop me from going out, though we do sometimes have to plan a bit more. I go to the pubs and clubs in Livingston like Chicago rock and Club Earth, and I also go out in Edinburgh to places like Edwards, Henry J's, the Citrus Club and Cav, though I tend to prefer pubs to clubs through there as it can be a long night, and I might fall asleep from all the drink. I've not been abroad since my amputations but I have been away for weekends in Glasgow and Newcastle upon Tyne, those were great trips and I managed them with little difficulty, though foreign holidays are something I would have to think a lot about as I have so many skin grafts and the sun is bad for them, I also have to keep them covered when it's sunny here"

Triple limb loss certainly hasn't curtailed Louise's love of having fun or enjoying a good night out.

"It can even be handy having the wheelchair for some clubs as they let my friends and I jump the queue" joked Louise.

Asides the pain and trauma and facing up to the fact that her life would be very different in some ways from now on , the low point after her operations was realising that some of the people she used to go partying with when she was able bodied weren't quite as good friends as she had thought.

"I really found out who my real friends are when this all happened to me, my real friends stood by me, those who didn't are no longer part of my life".

The flip side of that is of course that Louise knows who really cares about her now, and though that is undoubtedly a positive aspect of what happened to her, Louise cites another thing as being the high point in her recovery.

"It was when I stood up for the first time on my new leg. It felt great being upright again. When the time comes to try it again I'll be ready".

Though things have been difficult on the prosthetics side of things, Louise hasn't lost heart and is encouraged that advances are being made in that particular field all the time .

"Technology is changing all the time." One form of prosthetics that Louise doesn't need is a *prosthetic arm.*

18

"I tried one but to be honest I didn't really like it. I can manage fine with just one hand, though some things have taken a bit of practice. I can do my hair, use my mobile and do my make up with one hand."

Louise is currently single and lives at home, the family house having had significant adaptations made to parts of it so that she can get around more easily, these adaptations include a handy lift. Louise gets around the house using an *electric wheelchair* which she operates using a joystick with her remaining hand, though when she goes out she goes in a *manual wheelchair* as the electric one isn't very suited to folding up into the back of a car. There have been mishaps involving the wheelchair, though Louise admits that most of these were through drink after fun nights out.

"I once accidentally pressed the joystick when I was transferring and ended up being thrown forwards out of my chair. There was another time when I was petting one of the family dogs and I ended up falling out of the chair on top of it."

Thankfully, neither Louise or the dog were hurt on this occasion. It's not only amputees who have accidents and falls after a few drinks either though.

"I'm guaranteed a seat whenever we go out anywhere too" joked Louise.

Her love of partying and the fact that she has retained her sense of humour have been important factors in helping her get on with things.

Louise speaks very highly of all the medical care she has received since that incident in March 2005, particularly of the staff at St Johns where all her surgical procedures were performed.

"The help that I got was good, though the amputee facility seemed more geared towards older people, but that's understandable as most amputees are over sixty years old. I had good craic with the patients while I was in there too which was a big help and lifted my spirits."

GENERAL RATING OF NHS CARE: TEN OUT OF TEN

Louise's biggest inspiration in getting on with her life has been her family. They too have suffered in different ways after everything that has happened, which is perfectly understandable; no one wants something like this to happen to a loved one.

"My family have been amazing throughout everything, it's been especially tough on my brother William and my mum and dad but they've been there for me through everything. I wouldn't have everything that I have today, all the love support and security that I have, if it wasn't for them."

Louise drove a Renault Clio prior to the train incident and she hopes to get back driving again as soon as she can. A *driving assessment* has concluded that she will be able to drive an automatic car with a *push pull accelerator* with a special adaptation to allow her to operate it with her amputated arm side and an *infra red unit for indicating*. These adaptations are astronomically expensive though, particularly the adaptation that will allow her to brake and accelerate using her *residual* arm. Louise will be able to steer with a *steering ball* using her remaining hand.

"It's all about the pennies where driving is concerned, but I hope to be able to do that soon."

Driving holds no fears for Louise, just as much of life seems to hold no fear for her either. The only thing that Louise fears for the future is having to be overly reliant on others, and not being able to do things for herself that she has already re-learned how to do since her limb loss.

Prior to becoming disabled herself, Louise had an admirable attitude to disability which has stood her in good stead for what life has thrown at her.

"I never looked down on disability when I was able bodied, and it has helped that my mum used to work with disabled children in a holiday home called the Trefoil Centre, which is a holiday home for disabled kids on the outskirts of Edinburgh.".

Other people's attitudes have been mixed, though Louise hasn't singled out any particularly negative experiences.

"People who know me now know me for who I am and just treat me like Louise, which is what I want. Sometimes though, when we are out and about, other people can be unwittingly ignorant. They will ask whoever is pushing my chair all about what has happened to me rather than ask me directly. I feel like saying to them "HELLO. I'M HERE. YOU CAN ASK ME.""

That is quite common in society, though in most cases it's because the person asking is too nervous to ask the person in the chair in case the person has some kind of mental disability and won't be able to reply. No such problems afflict Louise though and attitudes are changing all the time, so hopefully she won't encounter this ignorance as often in the future. Louise has encountered similar problems with people staring, but she has the right attitude towards that too.

"I don't notice people staring at me anymore, and anyway, if they're staring at me that means they're leaving everybody else alone."

Admirably, Louise is now looking to get back into her old line of work, on a part time basis, and has applied for a few jobs that vary between ten and sixteen hours per week. Her old skills in that field are still there as she can still type, speak and use the telephone. Hopefully, Louise will find something that suits her soon. Longer term, she hopes to keep having a good social life, to learn to walk even if it isn't that far a distance and possibly to get her own house, though she is happy staying at home for the time being and is in no rush.

Louise regards herself as being a better person than she was prior to her limb loss, and sees that as a positive outcome of the last few years' tribulations.

"Before I was never at home, I was always out and about, now I appreciate my true friends and family a lot more and I think I have a much better outlook on life. I've never really cried about what's happened to me and the way I see it now, they were only legs, I'm still here, you just have to get on with it. If I wasn't the person I am there is every chance I could still be in hospital crying about it all.

New years Eve of 2005 was hard as I was not long home and didn't go out, I was a bit upset at that but I made up for it Hogmanay 2006 when I went out in Livingston with my friends Lesley and Paul."

Louise also admits that she doesn't take as many things for granted as she used to, and is very realistic when it comes to day to day life.

"I know that I can't just get up and jump on a bus to the shopping centre now and I also can't just wake up of a morning and decide I'm going to go somewhere and do something. I have to be realistic and plan things now, but that doesn't make things impossible, just a little more difficult, but you get used to it. It has opened my eyes a lot to life too and made my true friends even more aware of all aspects of disability. We notice just how many places still don't have proper wheelchair access despite the *DDA act*, and of course my friends know the best places to take me out now, places where there will be little or no access problems with my chair".

Louise is unique in this book in that she is the only person who has had the added problem of upper limb loss as well as losing a leg or legs. It doesn't take a genius to figure out the extra problems this can cause with things like transferring and pushing a wheelchair. The loss of her arm will mean learning to walk again may be a little bit harder too and it remains to be seen how things will develop with that in the future. But Louise has been upright before and wants to do it again. She may require more *corrective surgery* on her legs to get upright again, but that's something that she is both prepared for and used to. The 'break' from hospital will no doubt have given her a chance to have a look at the world again from a different perspective and gave her a better idea of how life is going to be from now on, whether she is successfully fitted with prosthetic legs or not. If Louise shows the same determination and exuberance in learning to walk again that she has shown in adapting to her new way of life then she will achieve anything that she wants to. Louise is just like any other young woman her age, she loves pumping dance music, going for a drink, Chinese food and spending time with her friends. That awful incident in March 2005 hasn't stopped her doing any of that, nor has it stopped her from trying to do other things again that a

22

lot of people take for granted or even complain about, things like working and driving. That in itself shows that life's not about how many limbs you do or don't have, but it's about your attitude and outlook. That's what makes you who you are. And Louise is just like any other young woman in that respect. Limb loss is no picnic, it's life changing, but it certainly doesn't have to be life ruining. Louise was dealt a bad hand, she has played it as best she could and has come up trumps, still leading as normal a life as possible. Anyone who suffers limb loss, being confined to a wheelchair or indeed any other obstacle in life should use her as an example of how to soldier on. It's pure and simple. Louise just got on with it.

RICHARD VALLIS

"Don't ask yourself what you can't do, ask yourself what you CAN do!"

In the fourteenth and fifteenth centuries, English archers decimated vastly bigger French armies in the Hundred Years' War by deploying a secret weapon. This weapon was simple, effective and above all, deadly when applied en masse. This weapon was the longbow. It was responsible for small English armies, made up mostly of lightly armed archers, winning famous victories like at Crecy in 1346 and at Agincourt in 1415. This weapon, and the well trained men who used it, so infuriated the French knights with their expensive armour that they issued orders that any captured English archer was to have the two fingers of his string drawing hand, the two fingers nearest the thumb, cut off. Amputated. So that they could never use a bow again.

Upon hearing about this threat, before going into battle, English archers would stick these two fingers up, making a 'V' sign, and raise their arm to the French, showing their defiance, as if to say, 'here are my two fingers, come and get them'.

During World War Two, British Prime Minister Winston Churchill also adopted this V sign, often making it during public appearances or when being featured on newsreels of the time. V for victory. Defiance. Perseverance in the face of adversity. The V sign became synonymous with the Allied cause, Churchill's rhetoric and infamous V sign playing a major role in keeping the allies' spirits up.

Nowadays the V sign is still an expression of dogged defiance. Of not giving up. It can even be construed as being insulting, depending on how it is used.

Nearly six hundred years on from when those archers showed their defiance to French knights at Agincourt, another archer is shoving two fingers up at a hand life dealt him. Except this archer isn't out to shoot anyone, nor is he walking around waving two fingers in the air. He has given life the V sign in a metaphorical but very real sense. This archer's name is Richard Vallis. He hasn't been threatened with the loss of two fingers, he's lost a leg though.

Richard Vallis is fifty three years old and lives in Penicuik, Midlothian, just outside Edinburgh.

Richard was a self employed tree- surgeon, running his own business. An energetic and physically demanding job, he found it to be an interesting and challenging occupation. It's also a vital job in the wider environmental context.

A tree surgeon is a professional who practices the management and maintenance of trees (generally in an urban environment). While trees provide many benefits, they can also be very large, heavy, and complex things that require professional monitoring and treatment to ensure they are healthy and safe. Richard's work with trees included planting, pruning, structural support, diagnosis and treatment of diseases, insects, or abiotic disorders, lightning protection, and tree removal. While some aspects of this work may be done on the ground or in an office, most of it requires the surgeon to physically climb the trees, using ropes, harnesses, and other climbing equipment.

Richard thoroughly enjoyed his job and running his own business.

In 1994 he started to get pain in his leg and pelvis. Not the kind of ailment that someone who done such a physical job would find helpful at all. That wasn't the half of it though. Richard was diagnosed as having *bone cancer*, in his pelvis. Because of the kind of cancer, *chemotherapy* and *radiotherapy* simply weren't options. Richard was in and out of hospital for two years, a two years that were for the most part full of dreadful chronic physical pain. One solution that surgeons came up with was to remove his pelvis in a procedure known as a pelvectomy. His own pelvis was removed and replaced with an artificial one, thus removing the cancer. The *artificial pelvic joint* they inserted did get rid of the cancer, but it didn't get rid of the pain in the leg.

"It was immensely painful to walk on."

Doctors tried various procedures and operations to get Richard's leg right, but all to no avail. He was still in chronic pain.

Finally, in 1996, it was decided that a full *hemi pelvectomy* was required, complete removal of not only the artificial pelvic joint, but of the whole leg itself. From having just got rid of the threat of Cancer hanging over him, Richard was now faced with the prospect of full amputation and being left with one leg. To many people this may have seemed like too much, they might have wanted to give up. But not Richard.

Richard is married and has been for twenty three years. He also has a twenty one year old son who was only nine at the time of his amputations. Richard's wife was, of course, supportive and understanding, but telling his nine year old boy how his dad would be going into hospital to have one of his legs removed must have been difficult in many ways. Richard explained to his wee boy what was happening in a very clear and positive manner though.

He told his son "I'm going into hospital to have my bad leg taken off, and when I get out I'll have a new one."

Such a positive attitude must have rubbed off on his wife and child too, as such courage in another human being would inspire anyone.

Having his leg amputated, though of course very drastic surgery, had one very positive effect for Richard. Almost immediately all his pain was gone, neutralised, the source of it having been removed. He had been on a host of painkillers while he still had his leg, but was off them within two days of his amputation. Even more remarkably, he was back behind the wheel of a car after a mere ten days, using adaptations that consisted of a hand controlled accelerator and brake lever, while he used his remaining original leg to operate the clutch. He still uses these adaptations today. His adaptations were done by *John Docherty* from Livingston, West Lothian.

Richard walks using a *fixed knee prosthetic leg* and one crutch now. The only medication he still takes are painkillers for his shoulder, as he inevitably gets a little bit of trouble from it from using his crutch, as someone with an amputation like Richard's who can walk uses the equivalent energy to that of an able bodied man carrying two people. The extent of the effort that would go into that is obvious. Richard also takes tablets for high blood pressure, but that is unrelated to his condition and commonplace among many men his age. This doesn't stop him getting around though, nor does it stop him smiling.

Richard , unlike many amputees, wasn't completely unaware of or unused to disability prior to becoming disabled himself, as he had been working with people with disabilities and learning difficulties on a voluntary basis since back in 1984, when he was able bodied, long before his illness and amputation. This experience was to prove vital to him, not only in rebuilding his own life and getting what he needed from the NHS and the 'system', but it was also to give him an even better insight into the lives of the disabled people he was helping. Not many people who work with the disabled are themselves disabled. This courageous man actually KNOWS what disability is like and this no doubt stands him in good stead when he helps others.

He was involved in founding the Lung Ha's Theatre Company in 1984, a company that has been one of the leading professional theatre groups in Scotland, providing opportunities for adults with learning disabilities to become actively involved in the performing arts. He is still involved with the company today, albeit on a much smaller scale. The group is run mostly by professionals and other volunteers now, but Richard still gets a warm reception whenever he turns up.

The group is based in the Eric Liddell Centre in Morningside Road, Edinburgh, and puts on one full show a year both in Edinburgh and Glasgow. They provide a great outlet for people with learning difficulties and disabilities to be creative, something they might not find as accessible elsewhere. The company also tours further afield from time to time.

Richard's philosophy regarding other amputees and people with other disabilities is simple.

"Don't ask yourself what you can't do. Ask yourself what you CAN do."

Concern for others doesn't just extend to the theatre group though. When Richard was diagnosed with Cancer in 1994 he also had to take the agonising decision to dissolve his tree surgery business. Not only was he seriously ill and unable to do the job he loved, he also had a number of people working for him to whom he had to convey the sad news that they would soon, through no one's fault, be out of a job. It's never easy making a colleague redundant at the best of times, but it must have been one more hassle that Richard simply didn't need at the time. Yet still, despite his own illness and the uncertainty, he managed to take the time to look around and find jobs for his old employees. Not many people would find time to sort out other people's problems like that when they are fully fit and healthy, never mind when they've been diagnosed with a life threatening illness and are facing possible amputation.

With an original height of six foot and four inches, Richard was home from hospital after his amputation in a mere two weeks, getting around one his one remaining leg with a pair of crutches. About three months later he was admitted to the now defunct and demolished Princess Margaret Rose Hospital on the south side of Edinburgh, to be fitted with a prosthetic leg. His new leg was two inches shorter, to compensate for his amputation being so high. It certainly doesn't stop him getting around though.

Richard now sees that the two years of pain he endured prior to finally having his operation did have a positive effect of sorts on his life. It gave him time to think about what he was going to do with the rest of his life, whereas many people who lose limbs through *trauma* have to deal with all of that at once, the flip side of this is that he had to endure those two years of pain and uncertainty. Both situations might make someone give up, in Richard's case it just made him more determined to keep doing things.

One thing Richard enjoyed was swimming. One of the first times he went swimming after his amputation, he heard a little girl commenting on the fact that he only had one leg. The same wee girl noticed him having a coffee in the pool's café after the swimming session, and she seemed gobsmacked as he was of course, wearing his leg. "Children staring doesn't bother me, it's only natural, they are inquisitive."

The lesson about the Hundred Years' War and the longbow at the start of this chapter wasn't just random twaddle. Eighteen months after his amputation, Richard took up archery, and became very good at it. He shoots from an adapted stool, though his targets are round static entities (known as 'the gold') rather than mounted French knights of course. Richard so liked the sport and became so good at it that he learned to be an instructor. He uses an old fashioned Yew longbow, not unlike those carried by English archers during the Hundred Years' War. The only assistance Richard needs is someone to go and retrieve his arrows for him. A few years ago he came second in the British Disability Sports archery competition, though these days he is more involved with coaching people with learning difficulties and disabilities than he is with his own target practice. One MS sufferer who Richard knows has participated in the *Paralympics*, while several more of his acquaintances are hoping to appear at the next Commonwealth Games.

Richard coaches at local mainstream archery clubs as well as with Lothian Disability Sport and Scottish Disability Sport. And he loves it.

Richard doesn't use a wheelchair at all, unlike many amputees.

"I put my leg on in the morning after breakfast and it doesn't come off until bedtime."

That alone must take strength of Herculean proportions. He enjoys the odd beer, glass of wine, or dram of whisky, but only in moderation, his alcohol consumption has neither increased nor decreased since his amputation and illness. He smokes a pipe but is not a heavy smoker. Though he still enjoys the same diet he ate before his amputation, Richard only eats about half the amount he used to, his favourite meals being healthy simple foods like meat with vegetables.

"I eat about half the amount that I did when I was a tree surgeon, as the physically demanding nature of the job meant I had to. I would literally pile my plate so as to get as much energy as possible. I only eat about fifty per cent of what I used to eat these days."

The lowest points for Richard post amputation were knowing full well that his mobility and consequently, his life, would never be the same again. The aforementioned dissolution of his business and telling his employees that they faced redundancy was also a low, which in itself is remarkable. The first low point is common in almost all amputees at some stage, but to be worrying about others at such a critical time in one's own life shows that Richard is a man who can see the wider aspect to life, rather than just focusing on his own immediate situation.

As to the high point post amputation, that's a simple one for Richard.

"Getting back behind the wheel of my car and driving again."

He has also been very lucky in respect of not requiring further amputations, though as he correctly puts it, "with it being a hemi pelvectomy there isn't any more they can take away anyway." The only further surgery he has required since was when his *gall bladder* exploded inside him, though this was unrelated to his amputation and can happen to anybody.

Wearing one of the two biggest prosthetic legs in Scotland on account of his height, Richard is an inspiring man in his own right, yet he cites the disabled people he has worked with since 1984 as the biggest inspiration in his recovery and rehabilitation.

"I was lucky to have worked with these disabled people, though I hadn't actually worked with any amputees. Seeing them getting on with things over the years prior to my own amputation was instrumental in me helping myself. I applied the attitudes and principles I had shared with them, to myself, and have benefited greatly from it." Richard always sees the person, not the disability, and that has never changed for him.

General rating of NHS care – seven out of ten.

Richard's family have been of enormous comfort to him, over the last thirteen years especially. His son, aged seven when his dad got ill and aged nine when he had his amputation, was even a mini celebrity at school when he took one of his dad's prosthetic legs in one day. Richard's wife was a nurse so she would have a bit more awareness of illness and disability too, meaning Richard has been able to draw strength from both of them. The only adaptations needed to the family home were a ground floor extension, meaning Richard doesn't have to go upstairs in the house, and the installation of a standard *wet floor shower room/bathroom*, something most disabled people have. Richard commented on his not being able to go upstairs in his typically funny positive manner.

"My son likes it; he has the whole upstairs to himself."

Richard likes many different genres of music, though he has more recently become interested in the music of Eric Bogle, originally from Peebles but who now lives in Australia. The singer writes a lot of songs, some of which are about Australian soldiers who fought in the Gallipoli campaign of 1915, where many men of the Australia and New Zealand army corps (ANZACS) lost legs. This singer tells their stories.

The effect on Richard's love/sex life has been minimal, he has experienced a few small problems common in people who have had such drastic surgery, but mostly things have been fine. Age catches up with everyone and limits them a little in that respect, whether they are an amputee or not.

Richard doesn't need to do any sports or stick to any kind of training regime, his walking in itself keeps him fit. He may have lost a leg back in 1996 but one thing he certainly hasn't lost is his sense of humour. When he was on the ward at the Princess Margaret Rose Hospital he had a good relationship with the other patients and nursing staff, which is in many cases vital in keeping up one's spirits. He even had a tee shirt printed with the hilarious logo "amputees can drive while legless" which raised some eyebrows and many a chuckle from both medical staff and fellow patients alike.

More humour was evident on one occasion when Richard was coaching his Archery students and a fellow archer who was blind roared with laughter when Richard suggested that if they went to the pub they would end up "blind drunk AND legless." It's true what they say; laughter can indeed be the best medicine of all. Another funny incident occurred when a neighbour moved in who had a prosthetic hand.

Richard joked to the man's spouse that to live in that area costs "an arm and a leg." Both sides thought this was hilarious. Richard's son Paul has been a Black Belt at kickboxing for some three years and is also an instructor in the sport. Once, when Richard chatted to his son's senior instructor, Richard told the senior instructor that he himself wouldn't be joining in with his spare prosthetic leg as technically it wouldn't be kickboxing, as he would have an unfair advantage if he bashed someone over the head with it!

There was no up and running *amputee visiting scheme* by the Murray Foundation at the time of Richard's amputation, indeed the foundation itself was only in its infancy. Richard himself has since become a volunteer for this invaluable scheme himself though. He doesn't do as many visits as some other volunteers do, but that's because not many people get the operation Richard had. He's still available to visit amputees as and when required. Richard also believes this invaluable service should be universally extended to all amputees and their families, to give them a batter idea of how life will be 'post amputation' and also to give them advice that medical staff, who aren't amputees themselves, though highly dedicated to their jobs, can't give nearly as well.

"I think the hospital visiting scheme and counselling for families should be available to all amputees, there were so many things that I was told by professionals I would not be able to do. Things like walk with less than two crutches, climb stairs, carry objects and walk at the same time, I've since learned myself that I can do two out of three of these things, contrary to what I was told."

Only another amputee in a similar position would be able to give a patient a better insight into what they will or won't be able to do. Non amputees can only give general advice or advice based on what they have learned working with others, which though beneficial in many ways, isn't as valuable as advice coming "straight from the horse's mouth" as it were.

Richard's hopes for the future are to carry on his good work with fellow disabled people, to continue to live life to the fullest of his capabilities and to hopefully avoid any medical conditions that may reduce or hamper his mobility, though, as a realist, Richard knows this may happen with age anyway. But age catches up with everyone ,whether they are disabled or not.

He would like to work on a project whereby a DVD will be released showing amputees doing all kinds of things with or without their *prosthesis*, as actually seeing people doing these things would obviously be of enormous benefit to new amputees, either by encouraging them to emulate what they see in the DVD, or to inspire them to try something else that they had otherwise thought they would be unable to do.

Hopefully when Richard eventually retires from archery coaching someone will carry it on to the high standard he has, and maybe even take it on to another level, without detracting from the original ethos of allowing participation and encouragement for all. He hopes the same will apply to the Theatre Group he helped found. He doesn't plan to give up on the archery for a while yet though.

As to fears for the future, Richard only really has one, and it's a common fear among amputees. Essentially it is the fear of losing further mobility, either through further illness or amputation, or through age itself. These fears are perfectly natural though, and are by no means restricted to amputees. Though they can be a little bit more of a pressing concern for those with already reduced mobility. Medical science is improving all the time though, advances are constantly being made, so there isn't any need to worry unduly.

Richard's biggest negative from amputation was adjusting to his new body image and reduced mobility, again, a common factor for many post operation. The positive outcome was that it finally ended the two years of agonising pain he had been in.

Travelling abroad is an area that many amputees understandably can be unsure or wary about, though Richard says, "It's all in the planning. If it's a long drive we have to stop overnight, and we have to make sure that where we're staying is all on ground level and flat as I can't really walk on rough ground." Sensible planning.

Richard 'challenged' himself in this way by going to Dublin barely a year after his amputation, as the theatre group he works with were putting on a show there. He drove across, using the ferry via the Stranraer to Larne route, and made the journey with little difficulty.

"The ferry had a lift to take me from the motor deck to the passenger deck and that deck itself was very accessible."

Richard also took the family on holiday to France, driving the whole way. An overnight stop off in Birmingham was necessary, and they crossed the Channel using the ferry once more, from Portsmouth to Cherbourg in Normandy, rather than using the Channel Tunnel. Again, they experienced little problems with this trip as it was all in the planning. They visited the museum in Normandy that commemorates the fierce fighting that took place there in 1944 during World War Two.

When I asked Richard the question, if he could give one piece of advice to an amputee in a similar position, what would it be, he replied "Don't ask yourself what you can't do, ask yourself what you CAN do!" He also added "listen to what the medical staff who care for you say, but find things out for yourself too if you can".

Richard Vallis is truly a remarkable man, and a fine example of how to cope with what life throws at you. Even throughout his own ordeal he concerned himself with the welfare of others as well as himself, and his "don't give up, keep living your life" defiant attitude has no doubt seen himself and his family through some stressful and hard times. The earlier comparisons with English archers from the Hundred Years' War and Winston Churchill's own use of the V sign should now be evident. Here is a man who has stuck two fingers up at cancer and his amputation and refused to let either beat him. He has survived, carried on helping others as he had before and has kept his sense of humour in spite of the cruel hand life dealt him. Here is a man to truly inspire anyone.

KELLY CUMMING: TAKING EVERYTHING IN HER STRIDE. UNSTOPPABLE

"Take life as it comes. Life really is too short to dwell on things. Have a positive attitude."

Take a walk around any university or college campus across the world and you are guaranteed to see at least one student wearing a Che Guevara tee shirt. Che Guevara was part of a motley crew of revolutionaries who overthrew the corrupt government of the former Spanish colony of Cuba in the 1950's. In the early stages of their campaign, Guevara and his followers spent a lot of time hiding in and trekking across the various inhospitable mountainous areas of the island, to avoid detection by government troops until they were strong enough to descend the heights and liberate the island. To many people across the world, Guevara is the quintessential revolutionary. Dogged, unswerving, perseverant and strongly focused. But that was in the 1950's - and he's not the only person with such qualities.

In 2008, another brave, determined and ambitious person will take to the hills of Cuba. Though this person won't be facing enemy troops, they will face the same hostile terrain, blistering heat and sweating jungle faced by Guevara and his men fifty years ago. This person will also be undertaking this trek using an artificial leg though, a much more challenging task. And a much braver undertaking. This person too is also perseverant, focused and courageous. This person is a beautiful young Scottish student named Kelly Cumming. And the last few years have seen her revolutionise her own life in the face of adversity.

Kelly is nineteen years old and was born in September 1987. She has lived most of her life in Westhill, near Aberdeen in the north east of Scotland. She attended the local high school and enjoyed playing for a local girl's football team.

In July of 2003, when she was only fifteen years old, Kelly went to see the doctor about some nasty pain she was getting in her right shin. At first the doctor thought the pain was being caused by a football related injury, but an appointment with a consultant a week later revealed some surprising and devastating news.

Kelly had developed *osteosarcoma*, an aggressive form of *bone cancer*, in the lower part of her right leg. A life threatening illness. A week later she was admitted to the Anchor Unit of Aberdeen Royal Infirmary where she received three intensive courses of *chemotherapy*. Kelly had known that an amputation was probable, probably a below knee one. Unfortunately though, the tumour was too big and a much more drastic and life changing above knee amputation was now deemed essential for her survival.

"At first I was very hostile to the idea of them amputating my leg as I had always been a very fit and sporty type of girl, and I was even more disheartened when I was told it was to be an above knee rather than a below knee amputation. I now see that it was necessary though, keeping my knee might have given me more mobility, but at the same time the cancer may have spread and I might not be here today. When I woke up I was very upbeat and was cracking jokes, my friends and family weren't sure if it was the morphine that was making me like that or not."

I suspect, after interviewing Kelly, that this was her own personality just as much as the morphine talking.

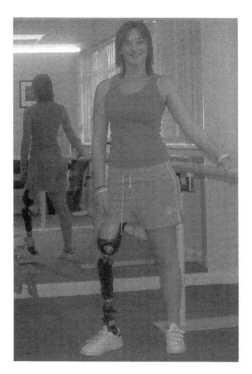

Kelly had this operation on the Sixteenth of October 2003, not long after her sixteenth birthday. At a time when most girls would be having a birthday party or making crucial decisions about career or further education, Kelly was faced with the prospect of living out the rest of her life with just one leg and with having a life threatening disease, a disease that she admits she had hitherto thought that only older people developed.

"I always saw cancer and amputation as being things that happened to older people. Of course I now know that cancer can affect anyone of any age, the disease does not discriminate. My only encounter with such diseases in young people had been when a friend of mine had died of *leukaemia* at the age of sixteen. I never thought that cancer would happen to me."

Sadly, it did, but although Kelly lost her leg, three more sessions of *chemotherapy* after the operation eradicated the disease and she was finally given the all clear from cancer in early 2004. Most girls of fifteen or sixteen's biggest worries are things like boys, spots and homework. In comparison Kelly had a monumentally dire situation thrust upon her.

"The *chemotherapy* made all my hair fall out and was also close to making me lose my hearing due to one of the drugs involved. I had to be given the *chemotherapy* at a slower rate because of this too, meaning that each stay in hospital was one night longer than most other people's would have been. One extra night may not sound like much but to me at that age it was an eternity".

Kelly was also given steroids that made her face puff up and was given a staggering nine *blood transfusions* in total. She became *anaemic* for a while and would oscillate between being a pale pasty white colour to being rosy cheeked and healthy looking during this treatment. She also felt very sick in general, particularly during the three separate chemotherapy sessions after her amputation. Remarkably though, she was out of hospital two weeks after her operation.

"I believe that I was discharged at the time I was for a reason. It was the beginning of a new year (2004) and I believe in fate."

To coin a phrase, new year- new beginnings, and this phrase is certainly appropriate when applied to Kelly.

Thankfully, not only did Kelly cope with it, not only did she survive, but it actually served to galvanise her in a way that she had never imagined. Kelly had been working part time as a waitress and even went back to waitressing after her operation, before getting a job in a local supermarket as a checkout girl.

"I went to work in the supermarket as the checkout was a job I could do sitting down, and as I'm naturally a people person I enjoyed it as I could talk to the customers". Kelly's career was soon to take off in another direction though.

"My life has changed so much since my illness and amputation. I went back to school and sat my highers but left school in May of 2005. I started applying for jobs with the multitude of local oil companies and sent my CV to Technip, an oil and gas company I wanted to work for who had a partnership with my local academy. I got an interview with them within two weeks and I am now a human resources administrator for them. I started with them in June 2005.

They have also put me through a degree in business administration at my local university and I hope to obtain my BA in 2008."

Kelly's job as human resources administrator involves giving new staff inductions and holding exit interviews with departing employees, dealing with staff pensions and general office work. The company has over seven hundred employees, so that in itself must be a very complex and demanding role, but it is one that Kelly thoroughly enjoys.

It's quite remarkable that anyone could embark not only on a new career, but also on studying for a degree, so soon after such drastic, life-changing surgery. Many people might have taken years to get over such an episode, but for Kelly, it seems to have been a mere blip, albeit a very serious one, that while having consequences, has helped her to focus on what she really wants out of life.

"I don't really see myself as having a disability; I see it more as I just have a prosthetic leg, that's all".

Kelly of course has had to make adjustments to her life though, as would anyone in a similar situation.

"My leg can get very hot and uncomfortable sometimes, and as it's a *suction socket* it can be prone to rotating, which can be annoying. There are some things I can't do at the moment like running, but I hope to be able to attempt that in future. I like swimming and have a gym at home to help keep myself in shape".

Kelly used to do disco dancing and tap dancing prior to her operation, and her younger sister has now taken over that mantle. Kelly also plans to have a crack at cycling and skiing in the near future if possible.

This is in stark contrast to how she felt around about the time of her illness and amputation, for a number of reasons.

"It didn't help that when I was diagnosed, the consultant spoke in medical jargon and didn't use the 'C' word. I was only fifteen, I didn't know what *malignant* meant, though I know this prognosis was as much aimed at my parents as it was at me. I also thought for a brief time that 'that was it', my life was over. I simply didn't know what I would or wouldn't be capable of doing from now on without my leg."

Kelly, in the last instance, is referring to the 'limbo' period common in all amputees, when they simply don't know what their mobility is going to be like if and when they are fitted with a prosthetic limb.

In the future when she has obtained her degree, Kelly wants to take some time out to go travelling around the world. In particular she wants to visit Thailand, Australia and New Zealand and North America. Many able bodied people would be daunted by such a trip, Kelly deserves great credit for aspiring to do this with a prosthesis. Kelly would also like to work at the headquarters of her current employer, Technip, in Paris, France one day too. No doubt she will stroll down the Champs Elise with as little trouble as she has gradually strolled through life since her amputation.

Foreign travel isn't a problem for Kelly either, and she has been on holiday with her family as well as going on 'girly holidays' with her friends.

"At first when my family and I would go abroad we would hire a private villa with its own swimming pool as I was a little bit self conscious about going in a public pool with one leg, but now I'm used to it we just go on more typical package style holidays. Travelling really isn't a problem."

Kelly wears her leg, which has a *hydraulic moving knee*, all day and doesn't use a wheelchair at all, in her own words "the one I have is currently in the cupboard gathering dust." She puts her leg on first thing in the morning and it doesn't come off until bedtime.

Thankfully Kelly doesn't have any other medical conditions and isn't on any long term medication for anything.

Her favourite food is a toss up between Chinese or a traditional Sunday roast. She doesn't have any special dietary requirements.

Kelly loves a good night out with her friends, like any other nineteen year old woman does, and she doesn't let having a prosthetic leg get in the way of that either.

"I enjoy a Long Vodka, a vodka and cranberry and also the odd glass of rose wine. On the weekends when I'm not studying we tend to go out to our local pub on the Friday night to catch up with everyone and see how they are all doing, then on the Saturday we'll either go out clubbing in town or go round to someone's house. I can still dance, though perhaps not in the way that I used to or would like to, and sometimes the flights of stairs in clubs can be difficult, but that said, my able bodied friends often complain about them too. Nightclub floors in particular can be very slippy, and I have fallen before, but people just assume that's through drink. I wear flatter heels than my friends so they often fall too when trying to walk in high heels. When I go out I tend to prefer the pub to clubs though as I prefer being able to talk to people and actually hear what they are saying."

One such night out ended with amusing consequences. After being walked home by a guy she had pulled, Kelly went home and woke up the next morning in her bed, with no leg at her bedside! Kelly's mum had found the leg, an expensive *cosmetically enhanced* one, out in the front garden of all places!

"I had walked all the way home from a twenty first birthday party some five miles away, when I woke up I was like 'where's my leg?'"

Kelly also has a 'party trick' where she holds up her artificial limb and twists it, reminiscent of scenes from the movie 'The Exorcist' much to everyone's shock/amusement.

Kelly doesn't drink excessively though by any stretch of the imagination.

Kelly's favourite music is dance and RnB, though she admits she is a little bit more open minded when it comes to music since her amputation.

"When I'm in the car I like listening to James Morrison, Beyonce and even Britney Spears".

Kelly learned to drive in an automatic as she was obviously too young to drive prior to her operation. She uses a *'flip' accelerator and break pedal system* in her Peugeot 206, though these minimal adaptations mean that others can drive her car, as and when required.

Kelly's low point throughout it all came the day before she had her amputation.

"I was so scared of the unknown. All my friends and family came round to see me the night before, but I was terrified then and even when I was lying on the trolley the next day waiting to go in for my operation. I just didn't know what to expect. I didn't know if I should perhaps take a photo of my leg before they took it off."

There were two main high points for Kelly throughout this stage of her life. The first one was simple, when she first got up and walked again on a prosthetic leg. There was another high point, amazingly, just before she had her amputation.

"I had been thinking a lot about what things I may or may not be able to do once my leg was off, one of these things was ice skating. I went ice skating for the last time with my friends and thoroughly enjoyed it."

In the broader aspect, Kelly was deeply touched by the realisation that she had so many people around her and supporting her, friends and family alike.

"It felt amazing having all my girl friends and family around me, and although they knew I was seriously ill they never treated me any differently, and they still don't."

Kelly's biggest inspiration in her recovery has been her friend Gavin Slesser. "Gavin lost one leg below the knee and one arm at the elbow in an industrial accident. He was twenty six years old when this happened to him. Despite this he is still a funny, outgoing guy who still goes out every weekend and has a great outlook on life. He has been a great friend and, to be honest, he makes it look easy."

Kelly also admits that she simply could not have handled everything without the support of her parents, Fiona and Graeme, and her sister Claire and her fiancé Jimmy, who put up with all her moods and kept her spirits up throughout everything.

Kelly and Gavin are both members of LOONS (Limbless Organisation of Northeast Scotland), a local support group and charity that allows amputees in the area to meet, share experiences and swap stories.

"It's great to meet with fellow amputees who may have the same problems as yourself".

Kelly is also a trained volunteer *hospital visitor* , having been trained by the invaluable Murray Foundation to go and see new amputees in hospital, as an amputee can answer questions that a doctor or nurse simply cannot. She does this through both the Murray Foundation, LOONS and her own GP. This kind of help from a fellow amputee is priceless to someone who has just lost a limb.

Love and relationships haven't been greatly affected by the last few years as far as Kelly is concerned.

"When I was diagnosed with cancer I had been with my childhood sweetheart for about three years, but it understandably put a lot of strain on our relationship, particularly as we were both so young, it was a lot for both of us to take in".

Kelly is currently single and having a prosthetic leg hasn't stopped her from leading a normal love life , though sometimes she avoids 'one nighters' as she can't be bothered explaining her story to someone every time she goes out. She's selective about who she sees in that respect. Kelly is quite right too, she's only nineteen, beautiful, funny and could have any guy she wants. Only an imbecile would be put off by her having an artificial limb. "Things haven't changed very much in my love life at all."

Kelly admits that she simply didn't have an outlook on disability 'before', as she didn't know anyone who was disabled themselves. Meeting people through LOONS and the Murray Foundation has helped her greatly in that respect, and her new awareness has even rubbed off on her friends.

"I have a friend who wasn't very aware of disability in the past and had a tendency to stare at people, I don't like it when people stare at me and I think this has had a positive impact on my friend, who tends not to judge people as much now."

Other people's attitudes can be less admirable though, and Kelly has been stared at or challenged in the past for parking in disabled parking bays (she has a *blue badge* and is perfectly entitled to do so). People must see this young good looking woman getting out of the car with no crutches and think "she's not disabled." That of course is a great compliment to Kelly, though the halfwits who do this need to take a serious look at themselves. Disability awareness in society is getting better all the time though.

GENERAL RATING OF NHS CARE – SIX OUT OF TEN

The only thing that Kelly really fears for the future is the unknown. But that is because she is so focused on doing everything that she wants to do that she doesn't want anything getting in the way of it. She wants to stay in control of her own destiny.

"I saw cancer and losing my leg as a hurdle. Anything else life throws at me will consequently be just another hurdle I have to overcome."

With such a positive outlook as this it's hard to see anything getting in Kelly's way.

In March 2008 Kelly will embark on a journey that most people would only dream of going on, and that many people would baulk at the mere thought of. Through the *Douglas Bader* Foundation, the charity set up by the late double amputee World War Two fighter

45

pilot, Kelly and twenty other amputees will be going trekking on the inhospitable terrain of Cuba. Ironically, Che Guevara first entered the mountains of Cuba with twenty companions too. On their second day in Havana they will visit Che's tomb. Day three will see them trek some eighteen kilometres. Day four will see them cover an astonishing twenty one kilometres over even tougher, steeper ground. Day five will see the party cover fourteen kilometres through dense woodland. On day six they will cover a further twenty two kilometres and on day seven they will walk another fifteen. All in all Kelly and her companions will cover some ninety kilometres in a matter of days, a remarkable achievement by any standards, let alone when accomplished by amputees.

"I'm really looking forward to challenging myself in this way. The way I see it, if the others amputees can do it, then so can I."

"I never thought I would ever say this but in a way I'm glad this happened to me back in 2003/2004. I've met so many new and wonderful people and it has given me a much clearer idea of what I want out of life. Of course I get bad days, but who doesn't? You just have to get on with things."

To say that the last three or four years have been monumentally challenging for Kelly would perhaps be the understatement of the century. Coming back from a life threatening disease AND losing a limb at such a tender age is a heartbreaking yet truly inspiring story. Not once during the interview did Kelly moan or complain about anything, and that's the way she seems to have lead her life since those dark days of late 2003. Not only does she work and have a vibrant social life, she hasn't forgotten how to laugh and is studying for a degree in her spare time. It makes light of some of the more trivial things that others complain about having to put up with. And on top of all that, she still finds time to help people who are in similar position through her volunteer work with LOONS and the *Murray Foundation*. Of course losing her leg at that age was tragic, of course she had a hard time of it, but if you meet Kelly all you will see is an attractive, intelligent, funny, smiling young woman with the heart of a Lioness. You get the feeling that Cuba will be, like everything else, just one more hurdle that Kelly will take in her stride. Kelly does indeed seem truly unstoppable.

Ian Colquhoun
(interview by Stevie Richards)

"I had a choice. Lie in my bed crying about it forever, or just do my best and get on with it. I chose the latter."

Drink, women and football. To most normal Scottish men under the age of twenty-five, these are three of the most important things in life. Their weekends often centre around either one night of pandemonium in a sweating hot nightclub filled with pumping music, scantily clad women and an endless supply of drink, or around a visit to watch their chosen team play, which usually involves an all day session in the pub. Unless of course, they are of the old firm glory hunting type who bleat on about 'their' team but hardly ever, or never actually go to watch them. Of course, a guy needs funds to participate in such a lifestyle, so most of those who indulge in a lifestyle such as this have to go and work monotonously for forty hours a week, just to get the money they need to have fun at the weekend and to survive midweek. One such man this rule applied to is Ian Colquhoun.

Born in 1978 and brought up in Livingston, Ian was quickly noticed by primary school teachers who told his parents he had the potential to be a genius, anything he wanted to be. None more so was in his talent for English and interest in history.

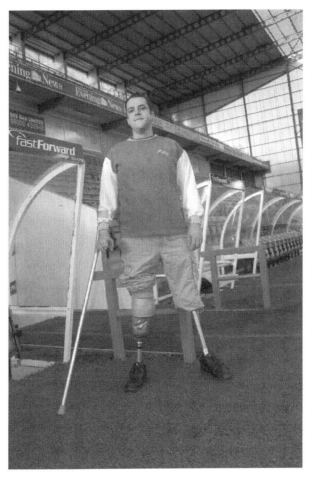

However, Ian quickly learned that if you're clever at school it can lead to unpopularity with fellow classmates, who would label certain clever kids a 'swat' or a 'snob'. Seeing how other bright pupils fell foul of this and having no such desire to be disliked by his peers, Ian soon started to use his intelligence and sense of humour both to wind up teachers and make his classmates laugh.

"My mum taught me to read and write before I even went to school so like some other kids in my classes I had a head start, I used to love to windup the teachers though and nothing made me feel better than making the whole class laugh in front of them at a silly comment I had made."

Now of course, he sees that kids who harass or name call others for being clever and good at their schoolwork are actually jealous of their abilities. But Ian's passion for windups and practical jokes was never to leave him.

"The best one in school was putting chewing gum into the lock of our modern studies classroom door every day for weeks, meaning we had to use a different room and couldn't get access to our paperwork, though they wised up to this after a while and just started to leave the door open, or get an increasingly irate school janitor to remove the gum with a screwdriver."

He had to move schools in the second year of secondary school and this, coupled with some personal problems, made him go into his shell a little bit, as well as giving him stress induced glandular fever for a considerable time. This hampered his education at a critical stage, particularly when it came to careers choices.

"I had wanted to be a journalist, but at that time I only wanted to be a Hibs fan."

One place where Ian felt free from all this stress was Easter Road Stadium, home of his beloved football team, Hibs. He was first taken there as a small boy by his dad but by his mid teens was attending games with various people of his own age , going on the east terrace, which later became the east stand, home of the more hardcore and vocal element of the Hibs support.

"I thought I was quite the big man at games, my mates and I would sing and shout and watch our team from that stand, and we weren't scared of ANY away supporters. It was our patch after all."

After a few crumby part time jobs after leaving school in 1994, Ian got a job at a local warehouse early in 1995. He worked there, and then in three other similar companies in the area for the next eight years. "The nature of the work was mind numbing for the most part, a monkey could do it, but it gave me money to buy CD's, clothes and to go out every weekend."

By the age of twenty, Ian was making enough money to move out of his mum's and share a flat with a good mate of his, his main reason for doing so he admits was "so I had somewhere to bring women back to after nights out."

Sadly, the next four years were to be a downward spiral. The partying and clubbing lifestyle, though great fun, took its toll on Ian mentally, and it started to affect his work. He had good friends but started to lose a grip on his finances, getting into debt. Despite numerous girlfriends and one night stands, he only ever loved two of them, and that hadn't worked out. All throughout this, his trips to see Hibs on the east stand and a few trips to Hampden were things he looked forward to. By the age of twenty four, he was in serious debt and his head was all over the place from over indulgence in alcohol and cannabis. Though he had managed to hold down a job for all this time, he felt like his only option was to move away for a fresh start. Having Irish ancestry on both sides of his family and being a Catholic, he chose the Republic of Ireland, a choice suggested by one of his friends.

"So many things hadn't worked out for me, the unfulfilling nature of my job was now making me unwell as I was now doing these jobs to pay off debt rather than to have fun with the wages, I needed to get away from the scene I was in, I needed to start anew."

Ian moved to Dundalk in the Irish Republic in August 2002 where he had got himself a job similar to what he had been doing in Scotland, but with a clean financial slate. Initially things went really well, he took to his new job and lodgings well, and made some friends, he even met a beautiful woman the first night he was there and things seemed to be working out, his gamble had paid off. He was even given a second job in a local sports bar by a fellow Scot, whom he had also met on his first day in the town.

"I loved the town, the people, and through my grandparents, I qualified to become an Irish citizen after a short time, and fully intended to do so."

Ian missed his friends, his family and his beloved Hibs, but in spite of this, things were going well.

The Scottish bar manager who had given Ian his extra part time job disappeared not long before Christmas ,and Ian was mysteriously sacked when this man disappeared, and though he missed having the guy to talk to about home and things, Ian's full time job and new friends made sure he could still lead a decent life.

On Christmas morning 2002, for no apparent reason, Ian was the victim of a hideous unprovoked violent attack after a Christmas Eve party, at the home of a girl he had been seeing for a mere ten days. He was beaten unconscious by two, possibly three people, and his attackers, assuming he was dead, set the house on fire to hide the crime, sabotaging the smoke alarm and jamming the doors of the house shut, so that if he regained consciousness, he would be unable to escape. Ian was going to die. Until one heroic member of the local Gardai (police) braved the blazing inferno to get him out.

All of his personal possessions like his wallet and mobile phone, as well as an expensive designer jacket he had just bought, were stolen after this attack. Ian was taken to the burns unit in Dublin's St James Hospital. His family and friends were informed by telephone, and through Scottish police, that Ian was going to die and they made their way over to Dublin.

Ian had went into a coma and awoke some seven weeks later. He had *full thickness burns* to his chest, abdomen, parts of his arms and, worst of all, to his legs. He also had complete renal failure, his lungs were full of black liquid, and his heart was failing. He also had minor burns to his upper arms, chin and hands. And a nasty head wound consistent with assault.

Ian's legs had to be amputated because they were so badly burned that all that was left was bone, and he could have died of gangrene had they not been taken off, though amputation by no means guaranteed his survival. He even contracted a rare Asian strain of the MRSA super bug whilst in hospital.

"I remember things about the coma, some were to do with my surroundings and can be explained, other aspects were of a spiritual or even supernatural nature and can't be explained."

One of the side effects of the drugs given to people in comas is that when they wake up, they often hallucinate or say strange things.

"I made lots of suggestive comments to the nurses that I was later embarrassed about, but I suppose they had heard it all before, they were lovely."

While Ian was in the coma fighting for his life, thousands of people all over the world were praying for him, thanks to the internet. When Ian eventually regained full consciousness, it was left to his mum and sister to tell him what had happened.

"At first I didn't believe them and believe it or not, I actually thought I should be signing myself out as I had work to go to, I asked for a pair of crutches so that I could go home. It simply hadn't sunk in."

When he saw his injuries for himself, when he eventually had the strength to lift his head, Ian cried and wailed like a child. Human beings are genetically programmed to be able to deal with the loss of a loved one, but the loss of one's legs is something the mind simply isn't designed to deal with. That night when his visitors went home, Ian just wanted to kill himself, but as he didn't have the strength and was still under twenty four hour observation, that was impossible.

"I initially hated my friends and family for signing the forms and allowing the doctors to take my legs away, I though it would have been better if I had just been left to burn."

These feelings, though perfectly natural, didn't last long though, as Ian realised that those who had signed the forms had had no choice.

" I understood after a couple of days and my attitude changed too. I had a choice. Lie in my bed crying about it forever, or just do my best and get on with it. I chose the latter."

As soon as consultants told Ian he would be able to get prosthetic legs, his mood improved even more, and within three or four days of realising he had lost his legs, he was regularly cracking jokes to his nurses and visitors.

His biggest concern when he awoke from the coma, amazingly, wasn't his legs, but whether or not he would be able to have sex again. Though he still couldn't move, he realised there was nothing wrong in that department when the MTV in his hospital room showed a sexy pop video, "all the things she said" by T.A.T.U.

"That made me realise everything was going to still be in working order in that respect."

Ian's face, bottom, back, genitals, neck and head thankfully weren't burned at all.

Everyone agreed that the best place for Ian, once he was fit enough, was back home in Scotland. Including amputations and *skin grafts,* he had had some fifteen operations and still needed two major ones, one to replace the black crusty burnt skin on his chest and abdomen, another far more serious one to cover a huge patch of exposed bone below his one remaining knee. Ian's left leg is amputated above the knee, the right one just below. He was flown home to Scotland by the Irish Air Force on the Eighteenth of February 2003, to the burns unit at St John's Hospital in Livingston, where he was to have those final two operations to his chest and knee, and from there, rebuild his life.

"It was a relief to get back to Scotland, not just because I knew someone had tried to kill me, but because visitors flooded in, everyone who had ever loved and cared about me came to visit."

Ian spent just over two months at St John's, where the plastics team worked wonders completing his surgery. The low point in that time was when a surgeon told him just before that all important knee op that "if this operation isn't successful you'll be in a wheelchair for the rest of your life."

Thankfully the operation, eleven hours long, was a success, surgeons covering the exposed bone below Ian's knee with a bit of muscle taken from his left forearm, and 'plumbing in' that muscle with an artery from his arm so that it could get a blood supply. This procedure is called a *bi scapular flap.* His other operations in St John's were also great successes, though the daily dressing changes were agony for Ian.

That April, Ian was moved to Astley Ainslie Rehabilitative Hospital in order to undergo rehab and be fitted with prosthetic limbs.

"At first I loved it there; it was great compared to being confined to one single room in St John's for so long."

Though he was fitted with limbs, a combination of *MRSA*, his wounds taking too long to heal, and the development of a bone disease in his knee called osteo- mylitis, meant that Ian was discharged from hospital in October 2003 without prosthetic limbs. During his time in Astley Ainslie, he had been rushed back to St John's for a further small amputation because of the osteo- mylitis, though thankfully that surgery and long term antibiotics have eradicated this problem.

Ian spent the next fifteen months in a wheelchair waiting to be re admitted to hospital to have the last operation he needed so that he would be able to wear his legs. He wasn't allowed back into St John's because of the MRSA issue at the time, though he himself was by now rid of the infection.

"I needed to do something, I was going crazy. Though I got a nice house in Edinburgh when I got out, I was bored, I needed something to do."

Ian started going to his local gym and doing upper body work, as he had put on a lot of weight having not walked for so long. He also started attending university on a part time basis, studying military history, one of his pet topics. It was on these courses that Ian's potential to be a writer and historian was again spotted.

Ian had a bad accident in 2004 at Hampden Park, when his team lost a cup final to Livingston. He was catapulted from his wheelchair after his wheels struck TV cables that shouldn't have been where they were, and to make matters worse he landed on his below knee stump, the stump that he needed the last operation on. Still, this did not expedite his return to hospital, though the severity of the wound meant he now needed drastic orthopaedic surgery rather than a simple skin graft. He eventually got this operation that he needed in

February of 2005, but he was in constant pain from when he had the accident at Hampden until well after his last operation.

The low point of the 'limbo' period, between being discharged from hospital in late 2003 and getting his operation in early 2005, was when he returned to Easter road and had to go in the wheelchair section of the main stand, as there was no wheelchair access on the east stand where he used to go.

"It was great to be back at Easter road but the atmosphere in the main stand was awful, like a library. No singing. I longed to get my new legs and get back on the east stand where I belonged."

Ian suffered some *phantom limb pain* after his amputations, usually when he was stressed, but he hardly gets any now.

His operation in February of 2005 was a complete success, and once his stitches were out, he went back into Astley Ainslie Hospital that summer. It was hard work doing the rehab, especially as the muscles he had used to stand and walk hadn't been used in two and a half years, but with his own determination and some fantastic help from his physios, slowly, but surely, he learned to walk again, firstly in parallel bars, then with a walking frame, and finally with crutches.

"It was an amazing feeling to be walking again. I had feared that because my stumps were skin grafted, that they wouldn't be strong enough to take my prosthetic legs, but the more I walked, the easier it got. When the physios showed me how to tackle stairs and I managed it successfully, I was elated, as I knew I would be able to get back onto the east stand in time for the new season. It was great being back on that stand, especially when we beat a hitherto undefeated Hearts two- nil. The atmosphere on the east stand was amazing, I was so glad to be back."

Ian walks with a fixed knee on his left side and has a *suction held leg* on his below knee side, with a Hibs badge laminated into the socket!

In 2004, Ian learned to drive using hand controls and now has an adapted car, the adaptations done by Alan Drysdale of Edinburgh. He continued studying part time until May 2006, and even did a couple of newspaper and magazine articles to get some much needed cash.

Ian's criminal injuries claim was rejected by the Irish Government as there was no conviction in the case. No one being jailed and receiving no compensation did upset Ian, but it didn't surprise him.

"My lawyer told me this was because of the Gardai, even the late Robin Cook told me that the force in the area where I was attacked are notoriously corrupt and incompetent, they aren't like our own police, sadly."

2006 was a good year for Ian. He appeared on a science programme called "Men in White" where the science team made him an attachment for his leg that included an iPod, disco lights, an alarm and a pedometer. Through the lovely producer of this show, Ian was also taken on by a specialist agency, *Amputees in Action*, who supply amputees to TV and film to add that extra bit of realism to action scenes.

Then that August, he got a publishing deal from Mirage books to release his autobiography 'Burnt', and getting that deal has opened the door to Ian for a number of other literary projects. He has since written a series of historical novels and is writing a number of books for charity, and hopes to continue writing long term, both as an author and as a freelance journalist.

Ian's scars are fading and in early 2007, *Amputees in Action* got him his first film role, playing a badly wounded sailor in a film called "Ocean of fear" filmed at Pinewood Studios, Buckinghamshire. "That was one of the most amazing experiences of my life; I had a spoken part and performed a dangerous underwater stunt."

Ian went through a terrible ordeal, but in a strange way his life now is better than it was before. He has finally gotten back to using his real talent, writing, and his family problems and drink and drugs problems are sorted out too.

"My life is better now, strangely, though of course, I miss my legs, dancing and playing football. My only other worry was that women wouldn't find me attractive but I've long since realised that simply isn't the case."

Ian stopped listening to dance music after losing his legs, but has rediscovered his love for it, though he listens to 'allsorts' now too. He is super fit and the 'man boobs' he developed whilst in hospital are now powerful solid pecs, with muscular arms and shoulders. He still goes to the gym every day, and is a lot more health conscious than when he was a 'drunken waster' back in Livingston.

His biggest inspiration in his recovery, asides from visits from Olivia Giles and Hibs striker Mixu Paatelainen, has been his friends and family, who he describes as simply "brilliant".

Ian's hopes for the future are now a lot clearer than they have ever been. Keep writing, keep walking, and avoid any illnesses which may hamper his mobility in future. He also wants to continue his acting and stunt work and his voluntary stints lecturing to physiotherapy students at Edinburgh's Queen Margaret University College. He would also love to settle down and have a family, but also admits that he has a lot of 'lost time' to make up for. He would like to go back and get a PhD to do with the Jacobite wars later on, and he also wants a crack at the TV show Mastermind, and has applied twice.

As to fears for the future, Ian fears losing his knee and the mobility problems that will cause, he is also afraid of further books he writes being rejected, but that one's a fear shared by all authors, not just Ian Colquhoun.

His amputations haven't ruined his sex life, though his experience in Ireland has taught him to be a bit more wary about whom he chooses to see.

Ian isn't bitter about his physical condition now, "people see me for who I am, if they have a problem with that then they're not worth knowing anyway."

General rating of medical care received – Ten out of ten.

Despite his problems before moving to Ireland, despite the unprovoked attempt on his life and despite all the pain and suffering he has endured, not only through amputation, but through painful burns treatment too, Ian is probably happier now than he has ever been. That is a tribute, not only to Ian's courage and determination, but to the human spirit and desire to live that is in all of us, if we choose to look hard enough.

JOE MCGUIRE

"DON'T LET ANYTHING BE A BARRIER"

Joseph McGuire, 49,   is a typical example of the traditional family man. A time served electrician by trade he has always held the admirable view that a man's role is to support and provide for his family. He has been married to Anne Marie for fifteen years and between them they have four children.

In 1996 Joe could not possibly have imagined how his life was to change, nor could he have envisaged that it would not only be his own family that would benefit from his support in the coming years, but a multitude of others too.

Joe started getting chronic pain in his legs in 1996, and a few months of medical tests revealed that this excruciating pain was being caused by a vascular illness, blood not reaching certain parts of his legs. Joe was naturally shocked by this, such illness usually being more inclined to affect older people.

"I thought this was the sort of thing that happened to people in their seventies, I was only thirty nine at the time."

He was put on *Morphine* at first until March 1997 when he had to have both of his legs amputated below the knee. Though this seemingly drastic surgery DID eradicate his chronic pain, Joe was unlucky enough to have complications whilst in hospital, predominantly a kidney infection that turned into complete renal failure. Normally in uncomplicated cases amputees can expect to be sent to a rehabilitative hospital to be fitted for limbs within six weeks of their operations, however, these complications made Joe's stay in hospital more like six months. Joe had never been seriously ill before in his life.

Luckily, he was fitted with two below knee prosthesis whilst in hospital so when he eventually got home in September 1997, he found he was able to walk around with little difficulty, even walking without any sticks or crutches.

The Murray Foundation was only founded in late 1996 so there was no up and running scheme where amputees could be visited by fellow amputees, though thankfully there is such an invaluable scheme now. That didn't stop Joe though, and he was able to walk round to the shops or nip out for a beer with little difficulty.

Limbs with attitude provided Joe with one of his first great experiences with fellow amputees, and the amputee sports days organised by the *Murray Foundation* gave him a chance to try out a multitude of sports and activities that he thought he may never have been able to do again. Amongst the activities he had a crack at were archery, rock climbing and bowling, all of which he thoroughly enjoyed. It wasn't just the activities at these events that helped and inspired Joe though; it was seeing fellow amputees participating too, even some of the instructors were amputees themselves. All this also lend itself to swapping stories and advice with fellow amputees and their families, something that, with the greatest respect, someone in the medical profession who isn't an amputee can't do nearly as well. Joe was also a keen swimmer prior to his operations so was delighted when he got the chance to get back into a swimming pool. He still enjoyed it thoroughly and even went a stage further after a while and learned to scuba dive! Amputation or limb absence could easily make someone a little apprehensive about doing such activities and sports, but there was no stopping Joe. He has even *flown a glider through a charity based in Fife* that offers the chance to fly a glider for as little as twelve pounds. That would take guts and determination for anyone, let alone a double amputee. He has also tried his hand at an adapted form of water skiing.

It was through *Limbs with attitude* that he first got involved in hospital visiting with the *Murray Foundation*, going to visit new amputees in hospital and answering any questions they have about prosthetics, rehab and things in general. It doesn't take a genius to figure out that such a visit would be invaluable to someone who has just lost a limb. There are so many things the new amputee worries about or is unsure about that can only be accurately answered by another amp. Doing these voluntary visits helped Joe too, as although he was doing very well with the physical side of rehab, the feedback he got from those he visited was of enormous benefit to himself too and helped inspire him to take things a stage further.

As an electrician, and rather a good one too by all accounts, Joe was of course worried about not being able to do his old job effectively and was concerned about the future and how he was going to support his family. Perfectly normal concerns for anyone who has had such life changing surgery.

"I looked into the future and saw the possibility of being stuck on benefits, having enough money to exist but not having anything with which to enjoy life, give the family treats or go on holidays".

Joe is referring to the '*benefit trap*' many disabled people find themselves in, where they are financially secure in the respect that they have a home, maybe a car and enough to live off, but that's it. And most jobs that disabled people can easily find can be low paid or mind numbing, and since they have to start paying rent and things like that, they can often end up worse off than they were on benefits, or maybe find themselves essentially working 40 hours a week, exhausting themselves and maybe only having an extra twenty pounds a week to live off. It's not, at first glance, a road that many would choose to go down. But it is by no means the only option open to anyone determined enough to pursue a different life.

Nevertheless, by 1998 Joe was walking with no sticks and people often commented on how they wouldn't have known he was an amputee as he was walking so well. The hospital visiting had shown Joe he had a talent that he perhaps hadn't noticed before, and taking that a stage further not only helped him in his own ongoing rehabilitation, it took him down a road he had never been down before.

A year long introduction to counselling at Strathclyde University was followed by doing a full time post graduate diploma in counselling at the same university.

"I had never been near a university in my puff before I undertook this."

Anyone on long term sick can study up to 16 hours a week without losing benefits, so this allowed Joe to complete the first access course without worrying about losing any money, this in turn opened the door to the post graduate diploma. During these two years he also did some voluntary work with a Glasgow based free counselling service for the public, in order to gain vital experience that textbooks and lectures simply can't offer on their own, and he did some work for a company that provides big firms with general counselling for their employees. Many big companies are now offering this help to their staff as a work based benefit free of charge as it is in their interest for their staff to be reasonably happy and focused. Joe now also runs his own *person centred counselling* business on top of all the other good work he does.

"A positive about what happened to me is that it has given my life new direction."

Joe is very happy in his new line of work and has found a common but very understandable factor within some of the new amputees he helps. The physical side of recovery and rehabilitation, unless there are many complications, can take care of itself with determination and looking after yourself, psychologically though it's a completely different ball game. There are many things new amputees worry about that Joe himself experienced. Questions like "will I be able to do this?" or "how do I go about doing this?" "What's it going to be like?" are all questions new amputees will ask themselves continually. Joe's advice is simple "ask, and try things. You'll never know unless you give it a go".

Joe suffered a further setback late in 1998 when a mysterious blood clot appeared in one of his *residual limbs*. The result of this was another amputation, leaving him with only one knee. This of course has potentially grave consequences, as it is much harder to walk with only one knee, indeed, only 1 in 5 double lower limb amputees (19% to be exact) can walk at all. This had two main consequences for his mobility and life in general. Firstly, steep slopes or large amounts of steps have to be either avoided or taken with much more care than they did when he was walking with both knees, and Joe now uses a stick to help him with his balance. Secondly, he has to use his wheelchair more now, particularly when going out for prolonged periods.

"I have to be careful and try and judge my outings a bit more, there is no way I could go into town shopping for hours just on my legs, you get to know your walking limits."

This is not unusual, lower limb amputees use much, much more energy than able bodied people do to walk, and having an above knee prosthesis is even more tiring and hard on the muscles. Joe still walks very well though, the first time I met him the only way I knew he was an amputee was because he was using a stick and because I knew I was getting a visitor with similar amputations to myself.

Some newly incapacitated people have big problems accepting the fact that they will need a wheelchair, but not Joe.

"I just see it as my transport when I use it now, it gets me from A to B when I need it, you get used to it."

Joe drives too using hand controls, which of course gives him an independence that he wouldn't have if he was relying on lifts or taxis all the time. Hand controls can be fitted free of charge on motability cars now and are very simple and safe to use.

Holidays abroad at first seemed a daunting prospect to Joe and his lovely wife Anne Marie.

"At first I thought we would be limited to holidaying in the UK only from now on, but holidays abroad are perfectly possible as long as you plan them properly."

Since his operations they have been to Cyprus, Florida and Las Vegas among other places. These trips have also shown Joe and Anne Marie just how differently disability is perceived in other countries, particularly the U.S.A.

Trying to hire a car with hand controls in Europe and the UK can be tricky but not so in America, though Joe owns a set of *Lynx hand controls* that can easily be fitted to any car he chooses to hire when away.

"The Americans have things sussed with disability in general, instant $500 dollar fines for ANYONE who uses a disabled parking space without a permit, ALL buildings have to have wheelchair access or they simply aren't allowed to open."

That is in contrast to the UK where some unscrupulous businesses get away with not having disabled access because they are a listed building. Shirking like that is not tolerated in America.

"I've found airport staff to be very helpful in general, though the first time I flew after my operations I was a wee bit nervous, America was again the best for this as all the connections and other transport needed are all sorted for you when you get there, they are really on the ball".

Joe admits that the wheelchair is useful in airports due to often having to walk long distances. Joe found the facilities on cruise ships to be second to none for disabled access too when he went on a Caribbean cruise, and has no difficulties with long haul flights as long as he can get an aisle seat to stretch his below knee amputated side a bit, hopefully without tripping up any cabin crew!

Finally in regards to holidays, Joe believes that as long as you plan your trip properly then you should have no more problems travelling as an amputee than an able bodied person does.

"It's all in the planning, don't be afraid, just plan it and go". The only places he would be wary of are the Far East and Africa as they won't have the access or infrastructure that other destinations have in place yet.

Celtic fan Joe still goes to the odd match at Celtic Park, the club operating a very generous policy of charging four pounds for the wheelchair user and four pounds for the carer. Most Scottish clubs have excellent policies for disabled fans, though the Taylor Report and the redevelopment it heralded in stadium design have also been positive factors in helping more disabled fans attend matches. Disabled parking is still a big problem at most clubs though.

Joe still really enjoys swimming and other activities and in 2000 he won three medals at a sports day, including one for club throwing, which is a variant on Olympic style events like shot putt and hammer.

"I still swim like a fish, my disability doesn't hinder me. I don't use special prosthetics for swimming though I did adapt some flippers once, maybe I should have patented them." Joe certainly hasn't lost his sense of humour.

Walking with a *3R80 hydraulic knee* on his above knee side, a knee that moves rather then being fixed, and a standard *iceross* below knee prosthesis on the other, with a pair of *flex feet*, it's not obvious that Joe is an amputee at all; it just looks like he has hurt his ankle or something. With regards to footwear he finds that the flatter the sole on the shoes the better, as often shoes with a different heel height need to be re-adjusted by the prosthetist. Changing shoes can be a fiddly nightmare, as can getting trousers over your legs, especially jeans. He can wear his limbs for up to sixteen hours per day.

The above might give the impression that it's been easy to move on from limb loss for Joe, he certainly has the spirit and determination needed to fight his own ongoing battle. But that doesn't make Joe devoid of fear or bad luck. Like most amputees he is worried about further complications down the line, particularly anything that might reduce his mobility still further, or worse, stop him from walking at all. Losing his remaining knee is a possibility that he is well aware of, and he is aware of how much that would hamper his walking, it's hard enough to walk with one knee, walking with two above knee amputations is even harder. Thankfully all is well on that front at the moment. Joe has been lucky in that he has only had one complication since his last amputation, a hernia, not uncommon in those who wear an above knee prosthesis,

"You use different muscles to move an above knee prosthesis, especially in your back, which can lead to back problems and things in later life if you don't look after the muscles in your *stumps* that you don't really use, that's how I ended up with the hernia."

Though he is a very busy man Joe tries to keep fit with swimming and visits to the gym when he can manage it, indeed when he was featured in an educational video for the *Murray Foundation*, you can see him lifting weights at the gym with an amputee friend of his. Joe still attends physiotherapy, whereas a lot of amputees' physio ends when they are able to walk and are sent home. Joe believes more amputees should consider persevering with physiotherapy after being discharged from hospital if they can.

Joe takes warfarin on a long term basis due to doctors not being sure where the blood clot that cost him his knee came from, the warfarin thins the blood sufficiently to hopefully prevent this from happening again. The downside of this long term medication is that it makes any stays in hospital last longer than usual, as nursing staff have to get him off the warfarin before they can perform any procedures, perform the procedure, then get him back onto it again. When he had that groin hernia in 2000 he was in hospital for three days, when an able bodied person without these complications would have been admitted in the morning and discharged in the afternoon after the operation. Nevertheless, he's had no trouble from that groin since.

Having lost limbs through vascular illness Joe is very conscious that things like poor diet and smoking, seemingly part of Scottish culture, will be a leading factor in many people's amputations. Re-education of people seems to be the key in preventing this from happening as much in the future, and Joe also thinks a fitness handbook for amputees would be of enormous benefit to those who could utilise it.

Joe himself has changed his diet in the years following his operations, although his favourite thing to eat is still a nice juicy steak.

"I've started eating more healthy GI foods, the kind of foods that go through your system more slowly meaning you aren't as hungry as often."

Foods high in protein are also high on his culinary agenda now, like the aforementioned steak and chicken.

"I try to watch what I eat all year, at least until I go on holiday, but who doesn't like to have a good feed when they are on their hols? I'm a little bit heavier than I was prior to my amputations but again, that's only natural."

Alcohol is something most of us enjoy, and Joe does too, though he doesn't drink as much as he used too.

"I used to drink like most guys, go out for a drink, sometimes a bloody good drink, but that's a bit dangerous now walking on two artificial limbs, it's sometimes hard enough to do that sober let alone drunk."

He still enjoys a drink at home with his wife or on special occasions though, moderation being the key. He honestly admits that drinking to get drunk out in town isn't the same with his new legs, but he's happy to limit his drinking now anyway. When he does go out for a "good bevy" he sensibly takes the wheelchair with him.

Joe never took recreational drugs before his operations and hasn't since either. "I've worked with and counselled a few people who have lost limbs through drug abuse and they sometimes get worse after amputation as the drugs are something they can still easily do that they could do before, but of course that invariably gives them other problems, most notably infection"

He has been very lucky with regards to *phantom limb pain*, a common phenomenon
among amputees where they can still feel their missing limb long after amputation, often very painfully. Asides a bit of pain post amputation all he has suffered in that respect is more of a phantom sensation, which is a lot easier to handle and as he says " is more like having an itchy toe that you can't scratch" rather than the agony suffered by some less fortunate patients.

There have been highs and lows since Joe's life changed back in the late 90's. Joe's low point was the uncertainty, the "psychological limbo" in between being prepared for limb fitting and getting walking again.
"I just didn't know what to expect, usually when something happens in life you have another life experience with which to compare it, I had nothing to compare this to, and the uncertainty was a little disheartening, a real low point was in rehab watching an older patient struggling between parallel bars with a single below knee prosthesis, I was thinking is that going to be me?"
These fears were understandable though. And of course at the time of his initial rehab there was no hospital visiting service from fellow amputees, no one to 'compare notes' with, as it were.

There have of course been humorous moments, most notably when Joe absconded from his bed at Stobhill Hospital in Glasgow to go exploring the grounds and visit the canteen.

"I knew I could just jump into my chair and zoom away, and I often did."

This often led to frantic phone calls from nursing staff panicking that they had 'lost' Joe, but he always returned of course.

As for the high point, that was when Joe first stood up on his new legs after six months of being on his back or sitting down.

"It planted a seed in my head that said I CAN DO THIS, and gave me the determination to press on and get walking properly again."

The euphoria of finally getting upright again spurred him on to complete his rehab and showed him that he COULD do it. Like most men, Joe found standing up to pee again was also a great feeling, something that most men take for granted.

Longer term, the most positive aspect of Joe's new life is that he finds he uses a lot more of his inner self, and as a consequence he gets a lot more out of other people than he did when he was an electrician.

Joe's biggest inspiration in the time of his rehab was mostly other amputees, seeing them getting on with things, swapping hints and tips and watching them walk. He also cites cardio vascular workouts that he does with a *hand cycle* at home as being instrumental in keeping him upright and healthy. Joe sees physical fitness as a permanent necessity for himself and recommends it to fellow amputees who are able to do so.

General rating off care from NHS – 7/10

Joe is grateful for all the care he has received within the NHS.

"There are so many good people working in the NHS, the only problem is money. There aren't enough prosthetists and not enough time is taken with each patient to make sure they are limb fitted properly. That's all to do with money though, pure and simple." A common problem within the NHS today and not the fault of the staff.

His family have been brilliant throughout everything that has happened, and Joe also feels that his family and friends have been made more aware of disability in the last ten years, as he has himself.

Joe's musical tastes have changed somewhat in the last few years. He used to be a big fan of rock and heavy metal, now he prefers swing and listening to big bands and great singers or "crooners" as he puts it.

"I now appreciate good music and singing now rather than heavy metal racket, but that change may well have occurred with age regardless of my medical conditions."

Joe admits that, like most people, he knew little about any disabilities prior to his operations; it was always something that happened to other people. And it's true, unless you know someone with a disability or are disabled yourself, then you are unlikely to know much about it.

"Children are great with disability I find, they will stare but that's only natural, they should be educated and made more aware of disabilities so they can learn how to deal with such things later in life."

Education is certainly the key in changing people's attitudes, young or old.

Self image isn't a big problem for Joe, though he admits he has problems getting suits to sit properly on him. "I could make a ten thousand pound suit look like a £100 burtons job" he joked.

Joe's hopes for the future are both realistic and admirable. He wants to research more aspects of limb absence.

"I want to keep doing what I'm doing, walk for as long as I can, keep working and above all keep helping people, I would like to think that I have made a difference." Joe most certainly has already. There is no doubt about that. Here is a man that has definitely bounced back.

JOHAN GRAHAM

Left in a corner to die. No hope of survival. Born without any legs and with a rapidly failing heart. There seemed nothing that Doctors with the unsophisticated knowledge they had could do. A baby girl left to die because of the attitude of doctors and serious physical disability. Sounds like a story you would hear on a TV advert today asking you to donate money to a charity that operates in the Third World. Sounds a little like a ghastly form of natural selection based on how people are born that was sadly common in certain areas of central Europe in the 1940's. This little girl wasn't born in the Third World, nor was she born in central Europe. She was born in the 40's though, in Glasgow, Scotland. She was given no chance of survival. She has recently celebrated her sixtieth birthday.

Johan Graham was given up for nearly dead by medical staff when she was barely a day old. She was born with *congenital limb absence*, different from amputation, but nevertheless it left her with no legs. Johan, though only a baby, surprised everyone when her tiny heart started to function properly of its own accord. Dr White at Glasgow's Yorkhill Hospital told Johan's parents that although it was unusual for a child both to be born this way and to survive, there was no reason why Johan wouldn't be able to live a normal life. If given prosthetic legs she would still be able to dance and skip, though she would of course have to work a lot harder to do so.

Despite her limb absence, Johan lived a normal childhood, though attitudes to disability in the forties were worlds apart from how they are today.
"In those days people's attitudes were that disabled people should be hidden away out of sight."

When the time came for Johan to start school she was initially placed in a special school, Holybrook Street School, one that catered both for the physically disabled and the mentally disabled. This policy in itself shows how ignorant and uninformed the attitudes of people within Scottish education were at the time.
Johan's parents and the minister fought tooth and nail to have her placed in a 'normal'
School, and after four years of pressure and requests the education authorities finally relented and she was allowed to go to normal primary school. The authorities' reason for this at the time was that Johan might have an accident at an ordinary school, but they relented on the understanding that anything that happened to Johan at this school would solely be her parents' responsibility.

Johan's primary school was Langside Primary School in Strathclyde and she attended this school with little difficulties, the only lessons that her disability excluded her from participating in were physical education classes. Other than the odd bit of ignorant name calling from fellow pupils, Johan breezed through primary school like any other child. The name calling, though saddening, is perhaps understandable as children can be cruel, especially when the attitudes of many adults in that day and age were little better.

Likewise, when Johan then went to secondary school she encountered little in the way of problems other than the occasional taunt from a fellow pupil. She was able to participate in physical education classes at high school too, though as she couldn't run she found her niche as the goal keeper when playing hockey, which she thoroughly enjoyed. A happy child who could do almost anything her peers could do, Johan had confounded not only medical science by still being alive, but also the negative and discriminatory attitudes of various individuals and policies within the education board.

"Things were very different back then. Peoples attitudes have changed so much thankfully."

Johan had required only one further operation and a few other visits to Yorkhill in the interim between her miraculous survival and leaving secondary school at the age of seventeen. This was when a kind of 'foot' started to grow out of the end of one of her stumps, caused by *bone spurs*, and these had to be removed. She was eight years old at the time. *Bone spurs* growing off the end of stumps are not uncommon in those with amputation or limb absence, and by and large they can easily be dealt with and cause no serious problems, though they can sometimes mean you can't wear your legs for a little while. Johan has one above knee and one though knee 'amputation'.

Johan got her first pair of prosthetic limbs when she was a year and a half old and describes them as being "like boots". She got these at Yorkhill Hospital but her further appointments were held at a unit in Glasgow's Sauchiehall Street that is nowadays The Savoy.

"I was lucky that the NHS had been created at that time, otherwise my legs would have cost my parents over one hundred pounds, which was a fortune in those days." Johan's first few pairs of legs were wooden with braces, as was common in those days. The visits to Sauchiehall Street weren't exactly ideal as not only was the journey to the place a fair distance, but the building itself where the prosthetics clinic was was a somewhat unclean dingy place, with old fashioned lifts and smooth tiles that are hellish to walk on with prosthetic legs . Most of the prosthetists were, to Johan anyway, really old men, but though she had little in common with them, she never had any real problems with them; one of them is even still alive today. The visits to Sauchiehall Street were an inconvenience though, as the wear and tear on a child or teenager's prosthetic limb, particularly someone as active as Johan, was inevitably going to lead to more frequent appointments. Growing up and outgrowing her limbs also made visits to the prosthetist more frequent, and Johan admits that this sometimes had a negative impact on her social life, having to cancel things because her limbs needed adjusting or replacing. It was a necessary occurrence though, Johan freely admits this. It kept her walking. The prosthetics unit was moved to Belvidere Hospital when Johan was a teenager and she admits "the facilities there were much better".

Johan first experienced really bad discrimination when she started to look for a job after leaving school. Her two dream jobs were being a hairdresser or being a nursery nurse, though these seemed impractical at the time and while they may have been rewarding, all that standing cutting hair or chasing about after dozens of kids made the possibilities of a career in either of these fields extremely limited, even if Johan had persisted in trying to get one of these jobs it was by no means certain she would get one, given people's attitudes at the time.

Johan's third choice was office and administration work, a much more sensible option and a field that she thought it would be much easier to find work in. Incomprehensively, Johan had great difficulty finding a job in this area too, despite her disability being no barrier to her competently filling an administrative role. She had countless interviews , all of which resulted in negative responses from prospective employers, not on the grounds of her being unable to do the work, but because she wore prosthetic legs.

"The excuses they gave were that I might not be able to manage the stairs or because I was disabled."

Poor excuses. No doubt Johan had to climb stairs to actually get to these interviews, yet this was lost on those who interviewed her. To Johan's great credit, she never let this deter her from continuing to look for work, and she got her reward when she got an interview with an insurance company called Scottish Amicable in 1963. The attitude of the man who interviewed her put those of the people and companies who had previously knocked Johan back to shame. When commenting on Johan's disability the man said "what difference does that make in this day and age whether you are disabled or not? We have lifts here."

Johan got the job and thoroughly enjoyed it, spending ten years there, and proving all those other potential employers who had been so negative and refused to employ her, utterly wrong.

1967 was a good year for Scotland. Scotland became unofficial world champions by beating the previous year's world cup winners, England, 3-2 at Wembley, a performance that has immortalised that Scotland eleven as "The Wembley Wizards" and showed the world the genius talent of Rangers legend Jim Baxter. Celtic also achieved great things in 1967, the famous "Lisbon Lions" becoming the first British team to win the European cup. 1967 was a good year for Johan too. That was when she met Ian, her future husband. The couple were married four years later in 1971. Ian is able bodied and is an electrician by trade.

"I never thought I would meet and marry such a wonderful man, let alone an able bodied one, I simply didn't think it would happen to me."

The couple have three sons, Steven who is now thirty four, Craig who is thirty and Kevin who is twenty six. Johan describes her sons as simply "perfect". Johan and Ian live in Dumbarton, near Glasgow.

Johan, though obviously delighted, had some concerns when she became pregnant with her first son Steven.

"The authorities in 1973 weren't like they are today. I was worried that they wouldn't think I was able to cope with looking after him, or worse still, might have him taken off me by social services."

In the end Johan's fears were unfounded, though she understandably did have some help from the local health visitor as it was her first child, though this is common with most mothers whether they are disabled or not.

Johan walks using limbs of a relatively older design, but this is though choice as she finds she can wear them all day and gets few problems with them. There is also the aspect of newer types of limb needing the wearer to maintain physical strength in their 'stumps' , and Johan with her busy active lifestyle simply doesn't have time to do the necessary physiotherapy for this. In any case, she walks everywhere and finds the limbs she has to be more than adequate for the task of keeping her upright. She can walk without crutches or walking sticks of any kind.

Five years ago Johan was trained to be a hospital visitor through the *Murray Foundation*, and now visits new amputees in hospital, an invaluable service that gives the patient the opportunity to ask questions of someone who is in the same boat as them, rather than relying purely on information from medical staff. Johan enjoys helping people in this way, and as well as attending WESTMARC and Gartnavel Hospital, she has been all over Scotland as part of this counsellor type role.

"I've been to Dundee, Edinburgh, Fife, all sorts of places and have met some lovely patients, people of all ages, it's been very rewarding."

1981 was the year Joan had her third son Kevin. 1981 was also the International Year of the Disabled. Johan's perseverance and determination to carry on living a normal life in spite of her disability were rewarded when in late December she won the prestigious "Woman of the Year" award from the Sunday Mail newspaper. She didn't enter this competition herself, she was nominated by someone, and Johan even refused a cash prize opting instead for something a little different...

In early 1982 Johan and her husband got to meet *Sir Douglas Bader,* the famous fighter pilot and double amputee at a golf club in Girvan, Ayrshire, where they had lunch. Johan herself was inspired by meeting this man, who walked on similar prosthetic legs to her own.

Douglas was commissioned as an officer in the Royal Air Force in 1930 but after only 18 months he crashed his aeroplane and became a double amputee caused by "his own fault" in an aeroplane accident in 1931. As a consequence of the accident Douglas was discharged from the Royal air force. He found work with the Asiatic Petroleum Company. After the outbreak of the Second World War, Douglas rejoined the Royal Air Force. Douglas was a member of 222 squadron and was then promoted to lead 242 squadron. His skill as an aviator and contribution as an outstanding leader and fighter ace during world war two, along with his continuous attempts to escape a prisoner of war camp after he was shot down, were immortalised in the book and film *'Reach for the Sky'*.

Having suffered a double disfigurement, Douglas has become an inspiration to disabled and able-bodied people alike by demonstrating the ability to "get on with your life". Post -war found him working for Shell, getting his golf handicap down to an extraordinary two and fund raising on behalf of many disabled groups and charities. Little wonder then that Johan found him to be such an inspirational character herself.

Douglas was honoured in 1976 with a Knighthood for his contribution and work on behalf of the disabled community, he died in 1982, an inspiration to all indeed.

That meeting had been a special surprise for Johan, and was one she will never forget as she had always admired the courageous and sometimes outspoken amputee aviator. He truly inspired Johan.

The Murray Foundation recently won a Queen's award for voluntary services and as a result of this Johan and Ian were invited to the Queen's annual garden party at the Palace of Holyrood House in Edinburgh 2006, along with Keith Ferguson and his wife. Keith is a similarly inspirational man who also wears two prosthetic limbs.

As this huge gathering involved rather a lot of walking and standing around, Johan sensibly took her wheelchair with her, though her chair is more like a trolley with wheels. Prince Philip, the Duke of Edinburgh, well known for his sense of humour and sometimes provocative outbursts, asked Johan if her chair was a 'Zimmer on wheels', to everyone's great amusement. The Duke then added that, given his age, he would probably be requiring a similar item sooner rather than later. Johan is another amputee who has retained a sense of humour throughout everything.

Things like meeting Douglas Bader and attending a royal garden party are just two of the things that have made Johan have a happy sixty years on this earth. All in all, despite her disability, Johan has no real complaints about her life.

" I've led a good life, I've been very lucky to have had three lovely kids and a smashing husband, and I've been lucky to have walked so much, you have to live life to the full if you can."

Johan sees herself as being fortunate to have been born without legs rather than having had legs then lost them through trauma or illness. That doesn't mean she doesn't wonder what having her own legs would be like.

"Of course I would just love to wake up of a morning, swing my own legs over the edge of the bed and stand up, but I know that's not going to happen and in any case, I'm used to the way things are".

Martin at WESTSMART is usually Johan's prosthetist, and she rates the service she gets from them as first class.

"I've never had any problems with them and whenever I need a repair or adjustment, they usually squeeze me in no problem, though I obviously have to wait a few hours sometimes."

The only problem Johan anticipates having with the centre in future is their ability to obtain parts for her old fashioned style prosthetic limbs, though that, for the moment at least, is thankfully not an issue.

Johan has of course seen sweeping changes to people's attitudes over the years as well as vast improvements in medical care and support. She has also seen so many more places become accessible to disabled people that were virtual no go areas when she was younger. She is very positive about these changes of course.

"When I was wee I struggled to get into a lot of establishments. I'm not saying that kids who are born like me nowadays are lucky, but they are fortunate to be born in a time when places are almost all easily accessible and peoples understanding and awareness of disability is improving all the time, for the most part. It's a far cry from people's attitudes thirty years ago."

Johan cites once such incident not long after she had her first baby when someone who knew she was an amputee actually lifted up the blankets in her son's pram to see if he himself had legs, such was this person's ignorance. Attitudes ARE changing though.

As Johan's limb absence was *congenital,* she obviously had fears that her condition would be passed on through her genes to her children or more importantly to any grandchildren she might have, as hereditary conditions tend to skip a generation. Thankfully Johan's sons have provided her with two lovely grandchildren, Darren who is four and Hannah, two, both able bodied, and her fears have proved unfounded, though they were completely natural fears to have.

So far you may get the impression that Johan's life has been easy, but that's only because of the positive outlook she has. Prosthetic limbs break from time to time meaning you need to use a wheelchair until it gets fixed, and of course Johan gets pain now and then from walking around all day on a pair of prosthesis. One thing that having limb absence rather than being an amputee has spared her is *phantom limb pain,* which is common in people who have had limbs amputated as their brain still thinks the limb is there.

"I don't get phantom pain as such, though I do still feel the odd nerve or muscle twitching in my stump which can be uncomfortable, but by no means unbearable. There will always be small problems and setbacks; the trick is to make the best of them."

Overall rating of care from NHS – 10 OUT OF 10.

Holidays and family trips certainly haven't been hampered by Johan's limb absence. When their boys were young, Ian and Johan used to take them to Rothesay, to a wee holiday home, with little or no problems.

In 1986 the family, along with seven other people, went on holiday to Mallorca, one of the Balearic Islands just off Spain. No problems at all either with the flying or with the resort itself.

"As soon as I got on to the beach that was me, all relaxed."

A trip to Benidorm wasn't quite as hassle free though. The travel agent made the place sound great but when they got there they found the hotel to be quite far from the beach and the terrain around it to be steep and full of inclines, not ideal for either a prosthesis wearer or a wheelchair user. They didn't let it ruin their holiday though, and like most disabled people who travel abroad, Johan advises that you plan your trip carefully and make sure where you are going has adequate facilities. The family still enjoy trips to Blackpool too. "It's great down there, all you have to do is jump on a tram." Johan's disability hasn't stopped her seeing a bit of the world.

Indeed, when Johan's limbs are in full working order, the only thing that can hamper her mobility is really bad weather like snow, ice or strong winds, but Johan puts dealing with that down to pure common sense. "I'll sometimes need a hand out to the car or that, that's about it".

Theatre trips can be a source of mirth to Johan and her friends, all of whom don't treat her like she is disabled, and all of them can appreciate a joke together. Seats in theatres such as Glasgow's Pavilion are often very close together and Johan sometimes gets her feet stuck under them, letting out a comedy "ouch" when this happens, to everyone's great amusement. Another funny moment occurred when Johan was in the Queen Mother Hospital and had her legs off and under the bed.

"The cleaning lady got a hell of a fright when she saw the feet sticking out from under my bed". Johan added "A sense of humour goes a long way."

Johan isn't on any long term medication relating to her condition, the only medication she takes is for high blood pressure, perhaps understandable for someone who uses so much effort to walk, but also very common in the over fifties anyway, regardless of whether they are disabled or not. Johan doesn't drink alcohol at all other than the odd glass of Bucks Fizz, and she doesn't smoke, which will help her to walk for longer and of course reduces the chance of vascular illness and need for amputations. Her favourite music is the music of Sydney Devine. Her favourite food is steak.

Ian and Johan have come across some jealousy and negativity in certain individuals. Ian, who also does voluntary work with the disabled now he is retired, cited abuse of disabled parking bays by people who have a badge but don't have the person the badge is for with them when they park in the space.

"You also get people who think that because you have a motability car you are loaded, they don't understand that you swap your mobility benefit for the car, I think these people would be shocked if they found out how little a severely disabled person gets to live on."

Johan described her family in one word- "wonderful."

"They've never treated me as if I'm disabled, though my condition has made them more aware of disability, which is of course a good thing. This in turn has rubbed off on my sons' girlfriends and wives, their friends, and our grandchildren, they know I need assistance from time to time, but they also know that if I need help, I'll ask for it."

Walking and housework tend to keep her fit, Johan used to go to the gym but found it boring as she could only do upper body work, understandable. She used to go swimming too, something else that her disability didn't stop her from doing.

As to the future, Johan naturally fears any illness or accident that may reduce her mobility or prevent her from walking altogether, common fears among most amputees, though ages catches up with everyone and doesn't discriminate.

Her hopes for the future are simple, to keep walking, keep living the life she has done, seeing friends, helping other amputees, seeing her grandchildren grow up, and above all to keep her positive attitude. Indeed, her only regret in life is that her own parents didn't live long enough to see her have children of her own.

Johan Graham truly deserved that award she won back in the 1980's. With the support of her friends and family, decent medical care and above all her own resilient spirit and attitude, she has overcame a lifetime of disability , being written off as a baby, the cruel attitudes of some fellow pupils at school and awful discrimination from prospective employers. Not only has she overcome this adversity, she is a loving wife, mother and grandmother who selflessly helps other amputees and those with limb absence. And on top of all that, she has retained her sense of humour. Inspiring is a word you will find a lot in this book, but it's used accurately in all cases, none more so than with Johan. One final word from her on the matter from when I asked her if she could give one piece of advice to someone in a similar situation to herself, what would it be?

"Lead as normal a life as you can. Don't feel sorry for yourself, get on with living." An attitude that would serve anyone well in life.

PAIGE: FULL OF LIFE

A police escort all the way from Fife, over the Forth Road Bridge and into an upmarket area of Edinburgh. Flashing lights. Blaring, screaming sirens, all at high speed. Normal road users having to move out of the way to let this high velocity mini convoy pass.

It could have been a big Hollywood movie star on their way to a premier. It could have been a politician or important foreign dignitary who warranted this special escort. But on this occasion the police car wasn't escorting a stretched limousine or Mercedes. The vehicle they were escorting contained a far more precious cargo than any film star or politician. Their destination wasn't a snobby hotel or glitzy meeting, but an Edinburgh hospital accident and emergency department. And the precious cargo they carried was a wee girl who was fighting for her life, and the wee lassie's distraught mother.

A healthy baby, born on time on October the twelfth 2001, after eight weeks Paige's health and weight started to deteriorate when she contracted a form of bronchitis, and her parents became increasingly concerned that she was not thriving and developing as well as she should have been, constantly becoming ill with things like colds and viruses. Nevertheless, Paige was walking by the age of ten months and had taken to it brilliantly. She quickly developed a love of dancing and was always turning the radio on so she could have a boogie in the house. Despite her earlier illnesses Paige was just like any other little girl of her age.

Paige's parents are Nicola and Barry Allan from Kirkcaldy in Fife. Barry is a landscaper and Nicola is a full time mother. In total they have five children, three girls and two boys. Sharri aged eleven, Jade aged nine, Paige is five, and two boys, John aged four and Liam, three. The couple have been married for twelve years.

One Monday while playing in the garden at her Granny's house, Nicola noticed that something wasn't quite right with her now thirteen-month-old daughter.
"She was playing away normally but I noticed that there was something different, something not quite right with her."

Paige was still not quite right when she was put to bed that night, but by morning it was clear that she was ill but Nicola had an appointment somewhere else with her then three week old son, so took the wise and sensible decision to take Paige to her Granny's until the other appointment was out of the way - her Granny could always call if things got any worse. And sadly they did. Paige's condition had deteriorated somewhat and she was both sweating and shivering, vomiting, and her hands were very cold. On hearing this, Nicola made an emergency doctors' appointment, but the soonest they could be seen was three o'clock that afternoon. The doctor, seeing obvious signs of some kind of viral infection in this ill wee girl, initially prescribed Calpol and Ibuprofen to be taken every two hours, but advised that if her "sky high" forty degree temperature didn't abate within eight to ten hours, urgent hospital admission would be required.

Paige's parents took her home and followed the doctor's advice to the letter, administering Calpol and Ibuprofen every two hours, giving her a bath, and doing everything the doctor had told them to do. Calpol , though effective in treating minor conditions in small children, brought down Paige's temperature, but at the same time this helped to mask symptoms of something far, far worse than anyone had imagined.

The next morning it was clear to Nicola that her wee girl was SERIOUSLY ill. It wasn't just the fact that Paige was now lying near motionless and had turned a very different colour, Nicola's motherly instincts made her see that something far worse than a simple virus was wrong, and Barry phoned the doctor again. Paige then took a fit and started having convulsions, naturally causing her terrified mother to scream and panic. These screams were not in vain and were heard by their new next door neighbour, who came crashing through their front door. By sheer luck this neighbour was a fully qualified first aid operative who took one look at Paige and advised her parents that they should dial 999 for an ambulance immediately. An ambulance was urgently requested and Paige's Granny was phoned to help with the other kids whilst this was all being sorted out. The ambulance took a long time to arrive, and when it did eventually turn up the paramedics told Nicola and Barry not to worry, that it looked like a viral infection, not uncommon in small children. By sheer luck however, there was a consultant paediatrician present at heir local hospital when they arrived, and he gave Nicola his view that Paige was showing symptoms of bacterial meningitis, a condition that the local hospital didn't have the facilities to cope with effectively. Paige was transferred by ambulance with the aforementioned police escort to the Edinburgh Sick Children's Hospital in the city's Marchmont area. Though in the meantime she was given vital fluids, Nicola feared that her daughter was going to die en route before getting the treatment she so desperately needed.

Paige's condition deteriorated in hospital to the point that her organs and other bodily functions were essentially being controlled by machines. Medical staff at first gave little or no indication about what the outcome would be, putting the family in a temporary limbo, not knowing something often being far worse than knowing how something is going to develop, for better or for worse.

Paige was in a coma for three weeks, her nose went black and her lips became a deep, deep shade of purple. No-one was sure what was going to become of her. All her distraught family could do was wait. During this time Paige's hands swelled up so that "they didn't look like hands at all", and her legs below the knee changed so much that they looked purple as if they had been recently *skin grafted.*

Paige had developed Septicaemia in her extremities due to the meningitis, in simple terms this means life threatening blood poisoning that starts in the body's outer parts (fingers, toes) then spreads, usually with fatal consequences unless the infected parts of the extremities are amputated. And amputation was now a necessity to save Paige.

Nicola and Barry had an awful but not difficult decision to make. Awful in the respect that no parent wants to sign a form authorising an operation that will leave their child severely disabled, but also not difficult in some ways as had they not agreed to this their wee girl would have died. It's a choice that no parent should ever have to make.

The surgeon, a genius of a man named Mr Quaba whom I myself have had dealings with , initially thought he would have to amputate Paige's arms above the elbow and her legs well above the knee, which would have left the wee lassie with severely reduced mobility for the rest of her life, but, using a process called skin washing, skin can be painstakingly cleaned and rolled back meaning that more of

87

the limb can be saved, so consequently Paige's amputations, though quadrilateral, weren't as extreme as they could have been, giving her a better chance of greater mobility for the rest of her life, though still leaving her severely disabled with two below elbow amputations and two below knee amputations. The procedure took some six hours in total and was performed a mere four days before Christmas.

Signing the consent forms allowing medical staff to proceed with the necessary procedures was one of, if not, THE hardest things Mr and Mrs Allan have ever had to do. But it HAD to be done. Naturally they were concerned about how their daughter would feel about their decision later on in life, as Nicola said, "I was worried that she might hate us for allowing them to do the operations."

I'm sure she'll understand when she's old enough to more realistically comprehend the gravity of the situation at the time.

Many new amputees who have their operations after *trauma* often get angry at the person who 'allowed' their limbs to be taken off, but this anger rarely lasts long, and the human desire to live plays a big part in this. In any case, the Allans have kept a scrapbook for Paige so that she can see how things happened for herself when she's a little older. It was obvious to me from the interview that Paige isn't bitter, nor do I think she ever will be, she's like any other adorable six year old girl.

People's reactions to what had happened at first surprised Nicola, and Nicola's own perception of things certainly surprised others.

"People couldn't understand how I was relieved at how the operations went, they were more inclined to say things in sympathy like 'but that's awful.'

Of course Paige's operations and situation were tragic, but at the same time so much more of her limbs were saved than had previously been predicted, giving her a much better chance of achieving things with prosthetic limbs, and consequently, with medical science making leaps and bounds constantly, this may lend itself to even better treatment in the future, treatment that may not otherwise have been available to Paige had the amputations been further up her limbs. And above all, she survived.

After two and a half months in hospital Paige was making really good progress but her parents were of course daunted by the prospect of Paige now essentially needing round the clock care , particularly as they of course have other children.

Paige ended up back into her local hospital again a few times with similar symptoms to what had went wrong before and, astonishingly, was twice sent home, her symptoms this time being attributed by medical staff to withdrawal symptoms from her medication. Only on the third return visit, when she again had a sky high temperature, was she re admitted, and Nicola panicked when she saw the charts on the end of Paige's bed.

"I recognised some of the names of things from the first time she was ill."

This time it was an E- coli infection that was causing the illness and it was thankfully caught in the nick of time. This infection, and all the ongoing medication, made Paige's teeth go a kind of see through for a while, and also affected her hearing, though for some reason it took the NHS some six months to arrange for her hearing to be tested, thankfully with no lasting damage.

"Paige was always the loudest, bubbliest of the four kids we had at the time and we knew she would be a wee star" said Nicola. "Barry and I knew she was a fighter at heart, and in a strange way we believe that's what has got her through everything."

To compound everything else, Paige's first set of prosthetic legs weren't really suitable as the feet were far too big, and to compound this there seemed to be some confusion within the authorities about who should be overseeing Paige's rehabilitation. Fife health board? Lothian/Edinburgh health board?

As a result of this almighty cock up, Paige was 'lost' in the system for nearly two years as no one department seemed to be focused on her care or supporting her family. For almost two years Paige's sole carers were her family. Nicola hopes this mistake won't be repeated again and that the NHS will have learned from it, at the very least so that it doesn't happen to anyone again. It would perhaps be a good idea for ANY person who has a severe lifetime disability requiring lifelong care and support to be assigned some sort of 'care co-ordinator' who manages everything to do with the patients needs, rather than having to deal with so many different people and departments, many of who's inter communication between departments is not up to scratch. That is a matter for the NHS though, though it's clear that a system like this would cut down on a lot of errors and bureaucracy, as all communications would be centralised through this one assigned care co-ordinator. Perhaps such a scheme will be introduced one day.

A positive of all these so far frustrating and demoralising events was an appearance by the family on early morning show GMTV. Paige's plight was picked up on by a private prosthetics clinic in England, a clinic who as a matter of interest made the prosthesis of Paul McCartney's ex -wife Heather. Paige got her first truly suitable prosthetic limbs from this clinic, which is famous not only for the mechanics of its products, but also for the realistic cosmesis which makes them look just like 'real' legs , right down to things like toenails and freckles, or hairs in the case of those designed for men. The legs Paige got used a *silicon liner* and were consequently very heavy. They were expensive too, as was travelling to England for consultations and fittings. No parent would begrudge such costs to see their child walk again, and the Allans also received help with this from the Meningitis Trust, but with their other children also to consider they realised they had to find an alternative.

This alternative came in the form of prosthetist Bill Spence who is based in Glasgow.

"He's been absolutely brilliant with Paige, first class, she's even had logos on her legs featuring things like Bratz, Winnie the Pooh, and love hearts, though there was a little confusion about the hearts thing, the prosthetist , perhaps jokingly, thinking Paige wanted a Heart of Midlothian Football club crest on her limb socket rather than love hearts."

Quite humorous considering the Allans are all Celtic daft (Paige's middle name is Erin). Prosthetists often offer to include such logos on limb sockets, not just for fashionable reasons, but often to lift the spirits of the amputee who is to wear them. And it's an approach that often works, the NHS do this free of charge if you ask them, in most cases.

Despite taking to her legs like the proverbial duck to water, Paige has required further surgery including an operation to remove *bone spurs*, almost like little shards of bone that threaten to keep growing outwards from the tip of the amputation and eventually break the skin. Fortunately, on this occasion there were no further problems as this was spotted early by medical staff and the family.

While visiting the Allans to write this piece I was greeted by an unexpected sight that brought a tear to my eye. Not only can this amazing wee lassie walk with prosthetic legs, she can also walk around the house on her stumps, which is extremely rare, exceedingly brave and, in short, inspiring to see. She took great delight in showing me what she could do walking around on just her stumps, using only furniture for extra support. Not many amputees can do that and this adorable brave wee lassie puts to shame a lot of people with lesser conditions who would maybe have given up. She doesn't do this to put anyone to shame of course; she's just a wee show off, like all wee lassies her age. And it's truly inspiring to see. She is also a wee chatterbox with a smile that would melt the heart of a statue. Her loving family and strong parents also deserve enormous credit for their wee girl's attitude.

A family friend, Olivia, also a quadruple amputee from meningitis/septicaemia, was amazed at how Paige can walk just on her *stumps*, for a lot of amputees this would be agony, or in many cases, downright dangerous. Olivia, who is also a good friend of mine, has helped the family a lot and is, in Nicola's words, "Paige's guardian angel."

Despite a few additional problems and the momentous task of having had to learn to walk some four times again, Paige has never given up and now wears lightweight legs that even allow her to ride an ordinary bicycle unaided, as well as ride a scooter unaided too. She also used a trampoline, more for physio purposes than for fun, but this trampoline was recently stolen in the middle of the night by what can only be described as ghastly cowardly sickos. Such vermin usually come to a sticky end though one way or another, there is a natural justice in the world in most cases.

It took a year of planning between education authorities and Paige's parents to develop a suitable personal care plan to allow her to integrate into class as smoothly as possible. This PCP package will be essential to Paige for the rest of her life in one way or another.

At the moment Paige isn't going to school, partly because of playground taunts about her appearance. Kids can be cruel and while this is wrong it can be perhaps understood in small children. However Paige's parents have found that when they have approached these children's parents to ask them reasonably to get their kids to stop it, that some of the parents are just as nasty and ignorant as the other kids themselves.

Barry and Nicola have even had warnings from the police just for trying to protect their daughter, which is frankly, disgusting, as has been the attitude of some members of Fife Constabulary, who are supposed to protect decent people like the Allans from sickos like this. Unsurprisingly, when Mr Allan offered to sort things out man to man with the chief adult bully and instigator, this cowardly wretch declined the offer as he is, like all bullies, a coward. And a pathetic excuse for a human being at that. A disgrace to our species. The kids who tease and sometimes torment Paige will hopefully become more aware of disability and see her for who SHE is as the years go on, for the sicko parents who allow their kids to do this with impunity, there is little hope. The crazy thing is, they themselves are only one illness or accident away from being in a similar position, such is life. Ignoramuses. The same adult vermin torched the Allans car, a blaze that was lucky it didn't spread to the house itself. Again, Fife Constabulary did nothing to help effectively.

It's not just her parents and siblings who stick up for Paige when someone makes a sick comment, on Valentines day 2007 Paige herself responded to a comment, coolly informing the child in question that " I've got my metal legs on and if I kick you it's going to hurt LOTS." Now THAT takes guts!

Paige doesn't use a wheelchair at all except when she was at school, using a special adjustable chair called a Wallaby, named after the loveable energetic inhabitant of Australasia, it's quite an apt name for Paige's chair in many ways. Paige is currently getting work sent home from school. She can write using a normal pen and was in fact one of the best writers in her class, quite a feat for a girl with no hands. She can even type on a PC keyboard and use a mouse without any special adaptations. She types using the tips of her arms' 'stumps' and seems unstoppable and able to adapt to anything. The only day to day thing that wee Paige has difficulty with is tying shoe laces, but that's easily solved by buying slip- ons or Velcro fastening footwear.

The only long term medication Paige takes is Melatonin, for periodic use to help her sleep from time to time.

The low point for Barry and Nicola after Paige's surgery, on top of the aforementioned fear that their daughter might blame them for allowing her limbs to be amputated, was the unknown, not knowing how well their wee girl, their other kids and indeed themselves would adapt to this monumental change in all their lives. These fears are common in amputees and their families post operation, but, it's clear that despite great adversity and some downright ignorance, the family have stuck together well whatever life has thrown at them since that day when the high speed convoy of police car and ambulance rushed wee Paige to the sick kids in Edinburgh.

There have of course been many high points during Paige's recovery and rehabilitation, one in particular was cited by Nicola, something that happened just after Paige's E Coli scare in 2002.

"Paige's food was put down in front of her, and she just automatically lowered her mouth to it and started eating it, without using her 'stumps', she also learned to put her dummy in this way, that showed me that she was going to be able to do a LOT of things for herself one way or another."

Late 2006 saw Paige's courage rewarded when she won two prestigious media awards for her bravery, one from the News of the World, one from Woman's Own magazine, both events having glitzy ceremonies in London. As well as receiving the awards themselves, and a load of toys which the actor who played 'Jonny Allen' in TV's "Eastenders" presented to her whilst disguised as Father Christmas, Paige and co got to meet Mylene Klass who used to be in pop band 'Hear'say' and pop Guru Simon Cowell, who sat and ate chips and ketchup with Paige while chatting to her for ages. Paige has also had VIP tickets to see girl band Girls Aloud and met the band too, with hilarious consequences. When the group's Cheryl Tweedy asked her who her favourite member of the group was, Paige cheekily replied "BRITNEY SPEARS!"

Paige wants to be a singer or a dancer when she grows up, and there is no reason why that will not happen, though at the moment her dearest wish is to learn to ice skate, though this is proving difficult in respect of finding boots that fit her prosthesis. Perhaps one of the problem solving TV shows like "Men in White" or "Braniac" will be able to help her achieve this dream, or perhaps there is already equipment out there that will allow her to fulfil this wee dream, it certainly doesn't seem impossible by any stretch of the imagination. If you're reading this and think you can help, contact the publisher! I'm sure Paige will be a great skater, she has the courage and right attitude to succeed, and with continued support of her loving family and people like Olivia I'm sure she'll be attempting figure of 8's before too long. Jane Torville eat your heart out!

This has been the hardest piece of literature I have ever had to write as I have been telling two stories in one that are of course, bonded and intermingled. It has also been a very humbling experience. But one I have also thoroughly enjoyed, it has helped me as an amputee myself.

Paige's lovely parents deserve infinite credit, not just for coping with all the hospital visits, NHS cock ups, uncertainty, callous victimisation and endless worry, but for the way they have stuck together in the face of such adversity and managed to bring up their other children too. I'm sure that while there will be further challenges for them in the years to come, not just regarding Paige, the last few years have given them an inner resolve that will allow them to cope with anything. They are an inspiration to any parent, in fact, to any decent human being.

As for Paige, from the moment I walked into the house she never stopped smiling or asking me questions, and she seems very aware of her condition, without letting it stop her doing anything. She knows she's a wee bit different physically from other kids, but that's the only difference. If you ever meet her, you won't see a quadruple amputee, you'll just see a beautiful, adorable child who is full of life and wants to do stuff that other kids do too. With the continuing love and support from friends and family, and with constant advances being made both in prosthetics and medicine in general, this amazing wee girl looks to have a very bright future, and with the right care and guidance, she could be anything she wants to be. Sure, she'll have growing up to contend with, but so do all other kids, and this kid in particular is truly a little star.

COLIN DUTHIE: WHY STARE? THERE'S NOTHING THERE!

"Whether you can wear a limb or not, stick at it and be who YOU are"

Hey, you could get hit by a bus tomorrow. How often do you hear that phrase being used by people when trying to encourage others to try something that they are perhaps unsure of or nervous about? It's a good analogy. Live life to the full and give everything a bash as you never know what's around the corner. Of course it doesn't just apply to busses. Lorries can be equally as dangerous. But not everyone who is hit by either vehicle dies, and not everyone who is hit by such a vehicle allows it to ruin their life. Colin Duthie is one such man.

Colin Joseph Duthie is forty three years old and has been married to his beautiful wife Julie for eighteen years. The couple live in Ayr and have two sons, Ian, aged fifteen and Stuart aged fourteen. Colin works as a sports development and equality officer for south Ayrshire council. They are an ordinary family in every sense of the phrase, but Colin himself came to find himself with this situation after an experience earlier in his life what was anything but ordinary.

Colin attended St John's primary school in Ayr and also attended secondary school in the town. He left school with no qualifications aged sixteen and got himself a job learning to install burglar alarms with Maxim alarms.

"I didn't have any formal qualifications, I got this job partly because I was going out with the boss's daughter at the time."

To all intents and purposes he was a normal young man, interested in women, fast cars, fast bikes and generally living life to the full and holding down a job. "I enjoyed the work, I really enjoyed it."

Colin's work, of course, saw him spend a lot of time going up and down ladders to install and service these alarms. Little did he know that his life was soon to be full of ups and downs of a far more, life threatening, life changing nature.

On October the fourth 1984 at around 8.32pm Colin was involved in a road traffic incident.

"I was on the back of my mate Jamie's motorbike, it was a beautiful October evening. Ideal conditions for a bike ride. We came to a new roundabout on the A77 and were going round it at about ten miles per hour. A guy in a white Fiat car suddenly pulled out in front of us forcing us to stop. My mate Jamie who was driving gesticulated to the car driver, indicating that we wanted him to get out of the way. The driver of the car just stared at us blankly, looking a little agitated. I remember glancing over Jamie's shoulder into the rear view mirror and seeing a huge lorry coming up behind us. Before I had time to look over my shoulder and implore Jamie to 'go', it was too late. The speeding driver of the forty tonne coal lorry lost control of his vehicle and hit us. The bike was catapulted up into the air and my mate Jamie was hurled over the barrier at the side of the road. I too was thrown off the bike and bounced of the barrier onto the road, thankfully unhurt at this stage. Then I tried to get up, lost my footing and slipped. As I lay on the road helpless I looked to my left and all I saw was the bumper of the lorry as it whacked me on the shoulder. I ended up underneath the lorry with my legs trapped in the exhaust and undercarriage. I was dragged along for a bit like this and my legs started to come off, then I got free of the undercarriage, only to roll out a bit to have my legs ran over by the lorry's wheels. My legs were pretty much mangled by this stage."

Eventually the lorry came to a halt and the driver leapt out of his vehicle to see what had happened. He was greeted by the sight of Colin lying screaming in agony, and the sound of Colin's mate Jamie frantically shouting "Gus, Gus!" (Colin's nickname at the time.)

Jamie, initially at least, was lucky, suffering only a sprained ankle and some bruising. Colin on the other hand was now in dire need of medical attention. He spent around an hour trapped under this lorry whilst the emergency services tried to rescue him. When they eventually arrived, after a time they had to use huge pneumatic balloon style equipment to pump the lorry up, so that Colin could finally be pulled free from it.

"When I was trapped under the lorry I was lying on my chest, so I could see that my arms were ok. I never lost consciousness for a second and I could still kind of feel my legs. It wasn't until a kind passer by who was 'rubbernecking' stopped and screamed 'oh my

98

god the poor man. His legs are off' that I realised my injuries were of a far more serious nature. There was no one else except Jamie around and I was the only one trapped under the lorry so I knew this lady who had stopped was referring to me. I remember thinking 'oh no, my legs better be ok, I've got work tomorrow'."

When Colin was eventually dragged free from the lorry he was taken to the local hospital at Crosshouse in Kilmarnock where, for a time, his life hung in the balance as he had a heart attack and was even given the last rites twice. His parents were informed of what had happened to him at about one am in the morning.

Colin was to spend some seven months in that hospital, undergoing over fifty operations of varying degrees of severity, and although his legs were horrendously damaged, they were initially still attached to him. These operations ranged from minor skin grafting procedures to the full amputation of his right leg well above the knee.

The amputation was initially supposed to be just above the ankle as gangrene had set in, but the procedure was changed to an above knee amputation as the gangrene infection quickly developed into gas gangrene, a far more life threatening variant of the infection that if not quickly dealt with would have spread up his leg and into his body, poisoning Colin's internal organs and ultimately his brain, which would have killed him.

"I had been in a coma for a week and was then transferred to ITU. When I regained consciousness, I was given two pieces of news by the doctors. Firstly, I was told that, thankfully, they would be able to save my life. Secondly though, they told me about the *gas gangrene* and told me that if I didn't have my leg amputated I would die from the aggressive infection. It was my decision. I was told I had to decide within a couple of hours what I wanted to be done. I lay agonising over this decision for a whole day, slowly getting worse and worse, edging nearer to death by the hour. All sorts of things were going through my head like:

'Will I be able to keep getting girlfriends if I only have one leg?'"

"I won't be able to run any more."

"Will I even be able to get a job?"

"Will I be able to drive a car?"

"If I'm not going to be able to do anything like this again I don't want to live."

All this time the infection was spreading.

Colin was also worried that he might be a burden to his friends and family if kept alive with only one leg and all the other injuries. These fears are common among those faced with limb loss, as was Colin's attitude at the time, particularly as he was such a fit and active young man who enjoyed running and martial arts, as well as the pursuit of women.

Though Colin left it dangerously late in the day before consenting to have his leg amputated, encouragement from his then girlfriend Julie (now his wife), his parents and his own inner resolve persuaded him to sign the forms authorising the operation.

"The ink wasn't even dry on the form when the anxious medical staff took me through to have my operation."

And so Colin's leg was taken off above his right knee.

This procedure was performed successfully, though this by no mean meant Colin was 'out of the woods' yet, not by a long chalk. Doctors soon became of the opinion that his badly mauled left leg would have to have a similar amputation; such was the severity of the injuries on that side. Colin's left leg essentially had no skin from his knee to his ankle and little or no calf muscle, his knee also had no patella or knee cap. Not only did Colin have leg injuries and an amputation to contend with, he also had multiple other injuries at the time such as broken fingers and other bones. He was, for a time, a physical wreck.

Six months in Glasgow's Canniesburn Hospital followed, where the most remarkable procedure was performed on him - and a revolutionary one at that. Colin's remaining leg was badly mangled and required skin grafting, but a treatment that had recently been tried for the first time on a HORSE was actually used to try and patch up Colin's leg. The procedure involves taking flesh and tissue and blood supply from another part of the body and making a 'flap', which can be surgically used to cover up any exposed bone or problem areas. This procedure is called a *bi scapular flap* and though it involved a lot of pain and suffering for Colin, the flesh, skin and blood supply taken from his back and grafted onto his remaining leg ultimately proved to solve the immediate problem and saved his leg. Colin was the first person to have this type of operation, which is now often used to 'patch up' trauma or burns patients. I myself had a bi scapular flap operation in 2003 to save my knee, and it ultimately made the difference between me being able to walk again with one knee or to struggle with two above knee prosthesis. If Colin hadn't agreed to this operation there is every chance that I myself would not be walking today. I didn't know this until I interviewed this brave outspoken man. Small world isn't it? Colin himself was very honest about his reason for allowing them to take the gamble with the flap procedure "I was probably going to have my remaining leg amputated anyway, so it made sense to give it one last go with this operation."

Curiously, this now standard, life changing procedure isn't named a 'Duthie' flap, after the man who it was first used on, but is instead named after the surgeon who came up with the idea.

Colin did get a respite from this stay in hospital when he was allowed out for his twenty first birthday party. Unfortunately, perhaps trying to do too much too soon, he fell down a big flight of stairs and hurt himself again, the main injury being the aforementioned loss of his knee cap. And so it was back to hospital for Colin.

Though Colin freely admits that being hospitalised did lead him to become a little bit institutionalised, it wasn't by any means a wholly negative experience for him.

"I met some of the most amazing and inspirational people I have encountered in my life while I was in hospital. Some of them were in a far better condition than me, many were a lot worse. I also attended rather a lot of funerals. I ascribe my own self belief to those hospital stays, they made me a stronger person."

Colin met his first truly inspiring fellow amputee at this time, a woman named Margaret, who at the time was eighty years old and had both legs amputated at the hip. Sadly she is no longer with us.

"She was amazing. She was in hospital having her fingers pinned straight so that she would be able to push her wheelchair and hadn't worn prosthetic legs since she was a child, but at the same time had led a normal life and had children and grandchildren. We even had a bit of an adventure one night when we sneaked off the ward to get a coffee. She went into the toilet but ended up getting stuck after actually falling down the toilet. I tried to help her but I was in a wheelchair myself with one arm in plaster so there wasn't a lot I could do. Eventually the nurses came to our aid and although we got a little telling off we were both able to laugh about it later, Margaret truly inspired me."

It is often the case that it takes another amputee to show a new amputee that they can still lead a normal life without their limb/limbs, and this was certainly the case with Colin and his friend Margaret.

Most of his operations attended to, Colin was eventually sent for physiotherapy and rehabilitation with a view to getting a prosthetic leg.

"At first I was daunted when I was asked to walk on a *PPAM aid*- (pneumatic post amputation mobility aid); it was like an electricity pylon with an inflatable unit inside that is used to give amputees their first taste of walking again. I was worried that my own new leg might be like this thing."

Those worries proved unfounded though, and Colin was inspired to see other amputees up on their prosthetic legs learning to walk again. Colin was assured that the prosthetics department at Belvidere Hospital would do their very best to make sure he was fitted with a prosthetic leg that was both functional and comfortable. They did do their best, but Colin's stump wasn't really suited to prosthesis because of the mauling it had taken in the road traffic incident. It just couldn't take the pressure. Nevertheless he battled away with his rehab and learned to walk again with an artificial limb. Colin beat the amputation. He proved he could walk again. He showed defiance to the cruel hand life had dealt him in the road traffic incident. But after a while he started to find that his new leg was giving him problems, chiefly with pain and with getting small infections from time to time. He persevered with the limb for five years before making what some would call a monumental decision. Colin decided in 2001 that he would rather get around on one leg with his crutches or by using his wheelchair rather than persevering with the prosthetics, that in his case had given him nothing but pain and hassle. He gave prosthetics a chance, a good chance, but decided one day to take off his new leg and never don it again.

"It wasn't a case of me not being cared for properly by the NHS or that, it was all about self perception for me. I was comfortable with the way I looked without my prosthesis, and my wife wasn't bothered whether I used one or not as long as I was happy. It's all about the person inside that matters, not outward appearances; it's not there, so why stare?"

Colin felt better almost instantaneously. To him, wearing a prosthetic limb was always about aesthetics rather than practicalities, but he's found that not wearing a limb hasn't adversely affected his life at all, if anything, it relieved him of the pain in his stump that was at times excruciating. That doesn't mean Colin doesn't like prosthetic limbs.

"Of course people should try to overcome their limb loss and get walking again, in a lot of cases getting upright on two limbs is a pivotal moment in a person's recovery. Wearing one just isn't right for me."

Whilst he has lived a normal life with just one leg since the day he finally cast his prosthesis aside, Colin is also open minded on the matter, and by no means rules out wearing a limb in future if one can be found that suits him. But he's not going to wear a limb just because it's the standard thing for most lower limb amputees to do. In that respect, although Colin chooses not to wear a leg, he is an inspiration to anyone who cannot be fitted with a limb for medical reasons. Colin is living proof that not having prosthesis doesn't necessarily have to be the end of the world for an amputee.

"It's a lifestyle choice for me; I find life easier without one, that's all. That doesn't mean that's what every other amputee should do."

Colin's outlook, though perhaps a little different from the others in this book, is indeed a personal one. But it should give heart to anyone who finds wearing a prosthesis too demanding, or to those who aren't able to wear one.

Colin's life has changed dramatically in many ways since that incident in 1984. He now works for South Ayrshire Council as a sports development and equality officer, primarily making sure that disabled children and young adults have as much access to sports and activities that able bodied people do. His work in the field of inclusion has had an enormously positive impact not only in South Ayrshire, but across Scotland.

His limb loss hasn't stopped him from undertaking other challenges either, and in 1995 he cycled across Israel with a group of able bodied cyclists, a daunting task in itself particularly due to the volatile political situation in the region.

"Thankfully there were two nurses in the group so I was well looked after, and I enjoyed whizzing along on my hand cycle."

Colin and his companions cycled some three hundred miles and Colin raised some five thousand pounds for the British Heart Foundation in the process. Colin has spent the last twenty years as a volunteer for many charities.

Colin hasn't experienced any problems travelling abroad for holidays either and has visited Croatia, the Algarve, Spain, the Balearic islands, Florida, Georgia and New York, with little difficulty.

"America is a great place for disabled people. There is no abuse of parking spaces there and everywhere is easily accessible. We got to skip the queue on the rides at Disneyland and were able to hire an electric buggy to travel around the park on. Skipping the queue for the fairground rides was a bonus, in fact as soon as I had finished on them I was asked if I wanted to go on the ride again, missing out the three hour queue. We even joked that we were going to start a website called 'takecolin.com' for people who wanted to get around such places faster without all the waiting". Colin might have lost his leg, but he hasn't lost his sense of humour.

Being completely comfortable with his appearance has also led to Colin being a mini media star in the past, having a part in the 1990 BAFTA award winning film 'Changing Step', directed by Richard Wilson, better known as 'Victor Meldrew' in the hit BBC comedy 'one foot in the grave.' Colin also appeared as a patient a couple of times in the TV series 'Dr Finlay'.

In respect of his career change, bike ride across Palestine and his media appearances, Colin admits that losing his leg gave him the opportunity to do these things that he otherwise would never have dreamt of doing.

"When something bad happens to you, you have two choices. You can see it as a disaster, as many people understandably would, or you can see it as an opportunity to take your life in another direction. Had I not been run over by that lorry I would never have been given these opportunities to have a positive impact on others lives, or to do these other things. Having a good and meaningful happy life doesn't have to consist of having good times yourself, it can also be about doing good things for others. Naturally I get bad days, but my philosophy on that is that a bad day can only last twenty four hours. And it's not just amputees who have bad days."

Colin has no other medical conditions other than high blood pressure, nor has he required any further amputations. He attributes the high blood pressure more to his love for Indian and Chinese food than to exerting himself because of his disability though. His favourite food is Steak. He doesn't really drink alcohol and is a non smoker. His musical tastes vary from contemporary smooth Jazz to eclectic rock like Led Zeppelin. Fitness wise, Colin is kept in shape by his walking, and he enjoys going swimming. He is however, glucose intolerant, and has recently been prescribed a form of anti depressants to combat his phantom limb pain, a common phenomenon in most amputees. He has had a few major medical setbacks in recent years, he recently crashed his cycle, breaking his femur on his stump side, but he has bounced back from that, just as he has bounced back from everything else.

Colin is also a keen horseman and has ridden for Scotland and Britain in dressage, his amputation hasn't stopped him doing that either. Colin drives using an automatic gearbox and no other special adaptations.

The lowest point throughout everything was around 1986 when it began to dawn on Colin that his life was never going to be the same again.

"At that time I could only see that my life was going to be different in negative ways, I couldn't see that it could also be different in positive ways if I had the right attitude."

The high points for Colin were realising that his wife loved him no matter what body parts he had missing and also the birth of his two sons.

"She is wonderful and loves me for who I am regardless. The only time my condition affects her is when she gets upset because I myself am in pain, as for my boys, I was told that due to my pelvic injuries I might not be able to have kids, my boys were born quite close together, in fact, for five weeks of the year they are the same age. So much for not being able to have kids! That's my high point, having a wonderful wife and two fine sons."

Similarly Colin's wife has been his biggest inspiration in dealing with everything, though others have inspired him too.

"It helps that Julie is a nurse but she is completely calm in the face of adversity and has been my rock throughout it all."

Colin has been lucky too in that his children, his friends, and their children have never treated him as being any different from any other man, and that disability awareness that they have shown has rubbed off on others. The only real negative incident came in the form of schoolyard taunts aimed at his children about their dad's disability, but when speaking of that, Colin added with a knowing smile "We soon sorted that out though."

GENERAL RATING OF NHS CARE: TEN OUT OF TEN.

The only thing that Colin believes needs to be changed in 'the system' is that amputees should be made more aware that it's not the end of the world and they haven't failed if they don't want to or can't be fitted with a prosthetic limb, and information about non -limb wearing should also go hand in hand with making sure that those who can be are fitted with a suitable one and receive all the necessary support. "Things are improving all the time" added Colin.

Colin is an outspoken, honest, tenacious man. His attitude to life is a great example to us all, not only of how to cope with the random nasty things that life throws at us, but also of how there are usually more than one way to solve a problem, if you are determined enough. Sure, Colin chooses not to wear a prosthetic limb these days, but he still went through all the rehabilitation, learned to walk again and wore a prosthetic leg for five years. In the end, it wasn't for him. Though he is a non limb wearer by choice, he is a source of inspiration to any amputee who for whatever reason cannot wear a prosthetic limb as he shows that life can indeed still go on. Likewise, people who wear limbs can draw comfort from his example that if anything happens to them in the future to mean they can no longer use prosthesis, they too may still lead as full and active a life as any other person. Colin Duthie is a fine example to us all.

Conclusion:

You have just read about how nine very different people have coped with limb loss or limb absence in their own, unique way.

Some, like Keith Ferguson and Johan Graham, have had problems since day one, and grew up in a society where ignorance regarding disability was rife, to the point of being accepted as the norm. Yet these two people soldiered on and have not only went on to live happy and fulfilling lives, they have actually found time to devote a big part of their lives to helping others.

Others, like Richard Vallis and Joe McGuire, were faced with limb loss while at the peak of their careers and while they had families to look after, which would have made adapting to their new life just as daunting at first, they too have got on with things and also do a great deal to help other people. Struck down by illnesses, both men could have crumbled, but instead they have shown inner resolve to keep leading as active and normal a life as possible, just as Johan and Keith have after their congenital abnormalities.

Colin Duthie proves that you don't necessarily need to use prosthetic limbs to live a full and active life, and, more importantly, he shows that there is hope for any new amputee who finds that for some reason they cannot wear prosthesis.

Ian Colquhoun (ahem!) appears to have used the despicable attack in which he lost his legs to carve out a new career for himself, doing something that he really should have done as a job all along rather than wasting his talent in warehousing. However, losing his legs did not galvanise him into taking up the pen, it was the need to earn and to survive that did that, as it does with most young men. And he hated writing about himself in the third-person perspective.

No one WANTS to lose a limb and it certainly shouldn't be seen as an option for lifestyle change. The people in this book have got on with life and have kept smiling because they HAD to, not because they chose to have their given situation thrust upon them. That takes nothing away from anyone's achievements though.

Kelly Cumming, struck down with Cancer at such an early age, has also showed great tenacity in both tackling her illness and in doing things that a lot of able bodied people wouldn't be up to, like trekking across Cuba. The mid teens are hard enough for girls emotionally without the added trauma of losing a limb.

The same can be said about Louise Mitchell. The incident in which she lost her legs and an arm was a bolt out of the blue, and although she has suffered and her life has changed, she readily admits that what happened to her made her open her eyes a bit more to life, and that, ultimately, it has made her a better person.

Paige Allan's story , from the outset, though heartbreaking, is both a tear jerker and an eye opener, as not only does it tell the tale of how this lovely wee lassie and her family have coped with the hand life dealt them, it also highlights problems at the time regarding care co-ordination. It also shows that, while most people's attitudes to disability have improved greatly since Keith Ferguson and Johan Graham were kids, there is still an ignorant element in society who can be downright nasty, though they are by no means restricted to harassing disabled people. Bullies are bullies. And nobody likes a bully.

Some factors are common in the nine lives you have just read about. Everyone has retained a sense of humour in spite of what's been going on in their lives, though it has by no means been laugh a minute either. They have all also drawn strength from family and friends.

Limb loss or absence is a 'big thing' no matter how you deal with it. But the underlying message of these mini biographies is that it doesn't have to be the end of the world, not by a long chalk. Whilst no one insists that limb absence has been a good thing for them, it simply hasn't stopped them from getting on with their lives; it has merely given their life a slightly steeper gradient than that traversed by most people. Yet they have all come out of the other side ready to face what life has thrown at them, limbs or no limbs.

When you get down to it, these nine lives, though at times heartbreaking and inspiring, have ended up being largely fulfilling and to all intents and purposes, normal. And that is the real triumph for all those concerned. Life goes on.

GLOSSARY

3R80 Hydraulic knee: The 3R80 was originally introduced 10 years ago and has been a popular choice for users who require a high activity knee joint. By revising the hydraulic swing phase control, the new knee makes it easier for amputees to initiate flexion for swing phase while walking at any speed. The new model accommodates patients who weigh up to 275 pounds, up from 220 pounds in the original version. The redesign also incorporates simple adjustment options and new swing phase control with progressive dampening

Advocacy pilot scheme: The Murray Foundation has been looking at the possibility of setting up an advocacy service to help people with limb loss deal with some of the problems and issues that arise in their life. This could be difficulties with benefits, housing, adaptations or community services – issues which for many reasons people sometimes find themselves unable to cope with. Beginning in April 2007 the Murray Foundation will initiate a one-year feasibility study to establish the need and format of an Advocacy service with a Murray Foundation volunteer working on the project one day per week.

Amputees in action: Specialist agency who supply amputee actors and extras to the TV and film industries .
E-Mail: admin@amputeesinaction.co.uk
Website: www.amputeesinaction.co.uk

Amputee visiting: Scheme where a new amputee is visited, usually in hospital, by a fellow amputee who had been trained specifically for this purpose. These visits are often invaluable to new amputees as they can ask questions about practical things that medical staff simply wouldn't be able to answer.

Anaemic: You get anaemia when you don't have enough red blood cells. This makes it difficult for your blood to carry oxygen, causing unusual tiredness and other symptoms.

The number of red blood cells can drop if there is:
1. a reduction in the number of red blood cells produced
2. an increase in the loss of red blood cells.

Artificial pelvic joint: Hip Joint replacement or Total Hip Replacement is surgery to replace all or part of the hip joint with an artificial device to restore joint movement prosthesis). Hip joint replacement is mostly done in older people. The operation is usually not recommended for younger people because of the strain they can put on the artificial hip.

The indications for the replacement of the hip joint include:

A.   Hip pain that has failed to respond to conservative therapy (NSAID medication for 6 months or more).

B.   Hip osteoarthritis or arthritis confirmed by X-ray.

C.   Inability to work, sleep, or move because of hip pain.

D.   Loose hip prosthesis.

E.   Some hip fractures.

F.   Hip joint tumours

This surgery is not recommended for:

A. Current hip infection.

B.   Poor skin coverage around hip

C.   Paralysis of the quadriceps muscles.

D.   Severe disease of the blood vessels of the leg and foot (peripheral vascular disease).

E.   Nerve disease (neuropathy) affecting the hip.

F.   Severe limiting mental dysfunction.

G.   Serious physical disease (terminal disease, such as metastatic disease).

H.   Morbid obesity (over 300 lb.)

Benefit trap:

i.   *Benefit trap: Incapacity claimants are afraid of reviews* – claimants are wary that looking for work would trigger a benefit review, which in turn can deprive them from their benefit - claiming status.

ii.   *Incapacity* benefit *claimants are wary of the financial implications of leaving benefits* – financial incentives are still quite limited for a substantial proportion of the claimant population. In fact upon entering employment a significant number of disability benefit recipients experience a loss or no change of income. Very few of those working 16 hours a week experience gains of more than £40 a week ,

iii.   *There is limited awareness of the existing return to work 'linking rules'* – claimants are wary of having to reclaim their whole benefits package, and possibly running into the same difficulties they had in securing it in the first place, if their job did not work out. Even those who return to benefits using the 'linking rules' have to have spent a further 28 weeks on benefit before the linking rules can apply again.

iv.   *There is limited awareness of the financial incentives to return to work provided by tax credits* – tax credits have a disability element that can improve the financial incentives for disabled people returning to work for 16 hours or more a week. However, awareness and take up among disabled people is low.

v.   *Permitted work rules for incapacity* benefit *claimants are restrictive* – People claiming IS can work under permitted work rules for four hours at national minimum wage without having their claim reduced. They often wrongly assume that they are restricted to working only four hours or they are discouraged to increase their work hours if they know they will not gain more than £20 for up to 16 hours work – the point at which Working Tax Credit kicks in. This perceived gap between five and 16 hours has been repeatedly criticised as undermining the flexibility of the system and disadvantaging those with fluctuating conditions who may not be able to easily progress to 16 hours work after they pass the four-hour disregard mark.

Bi Scapular flap: Procedure used predominantly on trauma patients, to 'patch up' gaping holes in the flesh that cannot be covered by a simple skin graft. Flesh and muscle is harvested from a healthy area of the patient and used to cover the wound. A minor artery is also taken from elsewhere in the body to 'plumb in' the flap and make sure it gets a blood supply.

Blood transfusion(s): Before a blood transfusion is given, the blood must be cross-matched to ensure that it is compatible with the patients' own blood. This involves taking a sample of your blood to identify your blood group, and matching it with suitable donor blood. This procedure ensures that the blood you are given will not make you unwell.

The transfusion itself involves a small tube, known as a cannula, being placed into a vein in your hand or arm. This is then connected to a drip. The blood is then run through the drip. Some people have a transfusion given through a larger tube put into a vein in the chest (a central line), or the crook of their arm (a PICC line).

Blood for transfusion is stored in small plastic bags. Each bag is called a unit of blood and is about a pint (half a litre). Transfusions usually involve giving 2–4 units depending on how anaemic you are. Each unit is given over a period of 1–2 hours. When the transfusion is finished the drip is taken down and the cannula can be removed.

If you need several units of blood you may need to stay in hospital overnight. However, a transfusion of only 1–2 units of blood can usually be given to you as a day patient or outpatient.

Blue badge: The Blue Badge scheme provides a range of parking benefits for disabled people who travel either as drivers or as passengers. The scheme operates throughout the UK. The concessions apply to on-street parking and include free use of parking meters and pay-and-display bays. Badge holders may also be exempt from limits on parking times imposed on others and can park for up to three hours on single yellow lines as long as they are not causing an obstruction (except where there is a ban on loading or unloading or other restrictions).

Bone cancer: Primary bone cancer is a very rare type of cancer and fewer than 500 people are diagnosed with it in the UK each year. There are several different types of primary bone cancer and all of them are rare.

Bone spurs: Small deposits of calcium, which build up along the edges of the bones. If they become big enough, or are further complicated by conditions such as impingement, they can become quite painful as tendons and other native tissues within the shoulder joint rub against them, causing inflammation and pain. A common problem in amputees.

Chemotherapy: Chemotherapy is a treatment used for some types of cancer Sometimes chemotherapy is used to treat non-cancerous conditions but often the doses are lower and the side effects may be reduced. This section does not cover the use of chemotherapy for conditions other than cancer. Chemotherapy is the use of anti-cancer (*cytotoxic*) drugs to destroy cancer cells (including leukaemia and lymphoma). The type of chemotherapy treatment you are given for your cancer depends on many things, particularly the type of cancer you have, where in the body it started, what the cancer cells look like under the microscope and whether they have spread to other parts of the body.

Congenital birth abnormalities : A "birth defect" is a health problem or physical change, which is present in a baby at the time he/she is born. Birth defects may be very mild, where the baby looks and acts like any other baby, or birth defects may be very severe, where you can immediately tell there is a health problem present. Some of the severe birth defects can be life threatening, where a baby may only live a few months, or may die at a young age (in their teens, for example).

Birth defects are also called "congenital anomalies" or "congenital abnormalities." The word "congenital" means "present at birth." The words "anomalies" and "abnormalities" mean that there is a problem present in a baby.

There are many reasons why birth defects happen. Most occur due to environmental and genetic factors. About 40 percent of all birth defects have a known cause. The remaining 60 percent of birth defects do not have a known cause. You may find it surprising that scientists and physicians have not determined the cause for all birth defects. This is why there is a lot of research into the causes of birth defects, to understand more about why they happen and how to prevent them.

Birth defects have been present in babies from all over the world, in families of all nationalities and backgrounds. Anytime a couple becomes pregnant, there is a chance that their baby will have a birth defect. Most babies are born healthy. In fact, 97 out of 100 babies are born healthy. Anytime a couple becomes pregnant, there is a 3 to 4 percent chance that their baby will have a birth defect. The 3 to 4 percent number is sometimes called the background rate for birth defects, or the population risk for birth defects. In a family where birth defects are already present in family members or the parents themselves, the chance for a couple to have a child with a birth defect may be higher than the background rate of 3 to 4 percent.

Corrective surgery: Operation(s) to rectify problems not resolved or made worse by previous surgery, or to correct any problems that have arisen afterwards or that may hamper the patient's recovery in the future.

Cosmetically enhanced: A prosthesis that is made to look more like a 'normal' leg through the addition of realistic 'skin' and sometimes even minor details like artificial toes and freckles.

DDA Act: Invaluable piece of government legislation brought in in 2005 covering many aspects of life including right of access to goods, facilities and services
For those providing goods, services and facilities directly to the general public, it is unlawful:
To refuse to serve a disabled person for a reason which relates to their disability.
For example: A pub refusing to serve a blind person on the assumption that they will spill their drink.
• To offer a sub-standard service to disabled people. For example: A restaurant asking a guide dog user to sit in a separate room away from other customers.
•

- To provide / offer a service on different terms. For example: A loan company insisting that a blind person consult a solicitor before being allowed to take out a loan, based on the assumption that s/he is less likely to have read and understood the terms of the agreement.

Further duties are placed on providers of services to make changes (called 'reasonable adjustments') so that disabled people can use the services more easily.

Degloved: Degloving injuries are the result of trauma to the body that causes tissue planes to separate. The more planes of tissue involved, the more difficult it will be to heal. In a closed degloving injury the skin may be abnormally loose as it lacks the normal connections to underlying tissues. Degloving injuries are often the result of an accident with machinery or a pedestrian struck by a car or other vehicle.

Douglas Bader: Group Captain Sir Douglas Bader, CBE, DSO, DFC, FRAeS, DL, became a hero and legend in his own lifetime.

Douglas Bader was born in London in 1910. Douglas won a scholarship to St Edward's School in Oxford. Followed by a place to the RAF College in Cranwell where he captained the Rugby team and was a champion boxer.

Douglas was commissioned as an officer in the Royal Air Force in 1930 but after only 18 months he crashed his aeroplane and became a double amputee caused by "my own fault" in an aeroplane accident in 1931. As a consequence of the accident Douglas was discharged from the RAF. He found work with the Asiatic Petroleum Company. After the outbreak of the Second World War Douglas rejoined the RAF. Douglas was a member of 222 squadron and was later promoted to lead 242 squadron. His skill as an aviator and contribution as an outstanding leader and fighter ace during WW2, along with his continuous attempts to escape prisoner of war camp after he was shot down, was immortalised in the book and film 'Reach for the Sky'.

On returning to England Douglas was promoted to group captain. He left the RAF in 1946.

Having suffered a double disfigurement Douglas became an inspiration to disabled and able-bodied alike by demonstrating the ability to "get on with your life". Post war found him working for Shell, getting his golf handicap down to an extraordinary 2 and fund raising on behalf of many disabled groups and charities.

Douglas was honoured in 1976 with a Knighthood for his contribution and work on behalf of the disabled community through the charity he set up, The Douglas Bader foundation.

The Douglas Bader Foundation was formed in honour of Sir Douglas Bader in 1982 by family and friends – many of whom had flown side by side with Douglas during World War 2. The mission of the foundation at its inception, and today, is to continue Douglas's work in conjunction with and on behalf of individuals with a disability.

The first initiative was realised in 1993 – the completion of the Douglas Bader Centre, a facility designed to support rehabilitation services for amputees built at Queen Mary's Hospital, Roehampton, in West London.

The centre provides a range of facilities and services for amputee members of the community, including a Walking School and Rehab Therapy Groups. Appropriately, this hospital had provided Douglas' medical care as an amputee for some 50 years. The Centre was opened by the Foundation's Patron, Diana, Princess of Wales, on February 25th 1993.

Working closely with all charities, associations and organisations that assist and provide services or products to amputees, they have joined-up the support and information services currently offered to best pool resources and serve amputees in the most efficient and purposeful way.

45 Dundale Rd
Tring
Hertfordshire
HP23 5BU
Fax: +44 (0) 1442 826662
email: douglasbaderfdn@btinternet.com

Driving assessment: If a person has a medical condition which affects thought processing skills then a driving ability assessment will be offered. The assessment includes an interview with the assessor (who may be a clinician or driving instructor) and may involve assessment of physical ability, visual assessment (ability to read a standard number plate from a distance of 20.5 metres and peripheral field screening), cognitive assessment (looking at the way the brain processes information) and a practical on-road assessment. Some centres have an off-road facility for those people who do not have a valid driving licence.

If the person's health condition only results in a physical limitation then a vehicle control trial or car adaptation assessment is usually appropriate. This includes an assessment for specific vehicle modifications which will assist with the control of the car.

Elective amputation: An operation that is the choice or decision of the patient or physician applied to procedures that are advantageous to the patient but not urgent.

Fixed knee prosthetic leg: Above or through knee prosthesis that operates whilst rigid, only bending when the user wants to stand up, sit down, or get in and out of a car. Often used as a 'first step' solution until the wearer becomes used to being upright again and is ready to try a moving knee, if suitable. What the fixed knee prosthesis lacks in flexibility it makes up for in stability.

Flex feet: special prosthetic feet for absorbing, removing pressure and stress from painful areas in the stumps. They promote the proper alignment of the feet, restore balance, improve sports performance and alleviate pain in the knee, hip and lower back. Orthotics are individually designed to correct foot imbalances and irregular walking patterns to improve the overall biomechanical function of the foot, lower extremity and entire body.

'Flip' accelerator and break pedal system: The system is designed with two throttle pedals fitted to the car which, in order to

meet new safety guidelines, are interconnected so only one pedal can be down at a time.
This means a driver can operate the throttle with the right or the left foot while the other pedal is safely folded up out of the way.

Flown a glider through a charity based in Fife:
Walking on air.
Scottish Gliding Centre
Portmoak Airfield
Scotlandwell
Nr. Kinross
Scotland
KY13 9JJ
walkingonairwa1@tiscali.co.uk
01592-840-222

Full thickness burns: Full Thickness burns are very deep into the skin. The skin feels very dry and hard. These burns don't have much feeling because the nerves (little things inside the skin that tell the body when it hurts) are damaged. These burns will not heal without an operation and are usually life threatening.

Gall bladder: The gall bladder is a small pear-shaped organ on the underside of the liver that is used to store bile. Bile is made in the liver and is stored in the gall bladder until it is needed to help the digestion of fat.

Hand cycle: Similar to a static exercise bike but operated by the arms instead of the legs. A handy home fitness appliance that usually allows the user to adjust resistance meaning that they can get a full cardio vascular workout without having to leave their home.

Hemi pelvectomy: is an amputation in which the complete leg, including hip, buttock and pelvis (at one side), will be taken away. Because of the consequences, the surgery is very rare (after the amputation, the patient cannot sit and lie straight up and walking with a prosthesis cost lots of energy). However this applies for all surgery, the more important for the hemipelvectomy is the mental and physical condition of the patient. He or she must be able to handle the new life after the operation. The 'classical hemipelvectomy', in which half of the pelvis is completely taken away, is hardly performed. The surgeon will try to save as much of the bone as possible, so that the bone can support the prosthesis. It is a plus if part of the pelvis of sit bone can remain.

Hemipelvectomy is mostly due to:

- Cancer (75 percent), mostly a sarcoma.
- An accident (20 percent),

Other reasons (5 percent)

Shortly after the operation, the amputee may and will feel unhappy, especially because sitting and lying is not comfortable, certainly not when the wound is still painful. It is often a comforting thing to know that sitting and lying will, as time goes by, in a week or two, gradually become better.

Hydraulic moving knee: A hydraulic fluid cylinder is installed in the knee that uses principles of fluid mechanics to vary the resistance of the knee as the user changes their walking speed. This allows the individual to walk at different cadences and have the prosthetic knee keep pace, ensuring the prosthesis is always in the correct position for safety when placing weight onto the prosthesis at heel contact. Hydraulic knee units are usually heavier duty than pneumatic knees.

Iceross: The Iceross Seal-In Liner is another major breakthrough in liner technology. It is a dramatically different and innovative suction suspension liner incorporating a hypobaric sealing membrane (HSM™) that provides a firm, comfortable suspension without an external sleeve. For lower limb amputees preferring a suction liner, liberation from the restriction of a sleeve offers substantially improved freedom of movement, increased comfort, and simplified maintenance. There are a number of different Iceross liners available.

Infra red unit for indicating: device that allows the person to drive the car and safely operate up to 18 of the car controls, one handed. Pressing a button on the transmitter sends a radio signal to a control box that is connected into the car's wiring. Most useful for any person who finds driving difficult with two hands, or who can only drive with one hand. All units can be used with either the right or left hand. Note that the keypad rotates to any angle, and can tilt towards the hand for easier use.

Jeff Gosling hand controls: Founded in 1988 they are now the market leader in hand controls for disabled drivers in the UK. Each system is tailored to the individual vehicle model allowing finesse of control and assuring the driver confidence and safe enjoyment of the vehicle.

Since 2001 they have been at the forefront in the development of secondary safety systems for hand controls.

Unit 3 Hollingworth Court
264 Stockport Road West
Bredbury
Stockport
SK6 2AN, UK
Telephone - (+44) 0161 430 2151
Facsimile - (+44) 0161 406 5020
Enquiries - info@jeffgosling.co.uk

John Docherty : Specialist car adaptations.

17 Herd Green
Fieldings
Livingston
West Lothian EH54 8PU
UnitedKingdom
Tel: (+44) 01506 435089
E-mail: John@docherty17.freeserve.co.uk

Laminated into the socket: Cosmetic work that can be carried out on a prosthetic limb socket, whereby the bog standard design is complimented by a logo or design chosen by the patient. Usually used to lift the spirits of a patient and to add a fashionable aspect to the limb. Artwork or pictures can be laminated into the socket as another way of customizing the "look" of your prosthesis. It's usually free.

Leukaemia: Leukaemia is a cancer of the blood and is the most common cancer in children, accounting for one third of cases. The term 'leukaemia' actually describes a group of cancers involving an excess of white blood cells.

In leukaemia, normal control mechanisms in the blood break down and the bone marrow starts to produce large numbers of abnormal white blood cells, disrupting production of normal blood cells and affecting the vital functions that these blood cells carry out.

Leukaemia can be classified as either lymphoid or myeloid, denoting the type of white blood cell affected. It is also categorised as either acute or chronic, reflecting the speed of progression.

Limbs with attitude: This is a unique event, which offers amputees of all ages and levels the opportunity to try out a variety of sports and leisure pursuits, under the guidance of trained professionals, some of whom are themselves amputees. There are thirteen different sporting activities, from cycling to tennis, sub aqua to Tai Chi, in a safe and instructional environment. Activities are geared at amputees of all levels of mobility, and age should not be considered a barrier. Run by the Murray foundation.

Lynx hand controls: a fully interchangeable hand control which will fit over 95% of automatic cars, taking just 5 minutes to install and 30 seconds to dismantle. This means you can use LYNX controls on courtesy cars, hire cars and for test driving These controls are only suitable for those with a lower limb disability.
Lynx Hand Controls
80 Church Lane

Aughton
Nr Ormskirk
Lancashire
L39 6SB
UK
Tel: +44 (0)1695 422 622
Fax: +44 (0)1695 422 152
Email: info@lynxcontrols.com

Malignant: Malignant tumours can invade and destroy nearby tissue and spread to other parts of the body.

Morphine: painkiller There are lots of different types of morphine that can be given in different ways, including
* An 'immediate release' liquid or tablet that you take every 2 - 4 hours
* A 'slow release' tablet or capsule that you take every 12 hours
* A liquid that can be injected into a vein or given through a drip
* A liquid that can be given through a small needle under the skin

When a patient starts on morphine, they will normally be given the more short acting immediate release type, which they take at least every four hours. That way the dose can be adjusted quickly and easily until they are comfortable. Your doctor or nurse will give you instructions on how much morphine to take and when to take it. Their instructions will allow the patient some flexibility so that they can take enough to control their pain. If the dose they are on is not enough for them, they will probably find that they need to top it up more often than 4 hourly. Keep a note of how much you have and when. Then your doctor can work out how much is needed every twenty- four hours. It is best to have an experienced Macmillan or symptom control nurse to help you through this process.

Once you and your nurse know how much morphine you need to get your pain under control, your doctor can give you slow release tablets containing enough morphine to control your pain for twelve hours. You take these twice a day - morning and night. These are sometimes called 'sustained release' morphine or 'MST'. The morphine is released slowly from the tablet and controls your pain for long periods. This gives you better pain control.

Murray Foundation: The Murray Foundation was established in 1996 by Sir David Murray as a support service for those affected by limb loss or absence in Scotland. Since that time the range of help and support offered has grown to incorporate the many different aspects of rehabilitation.

The Murray Foundation
9 Charlotte Square
Edinburgh, EH2 4DR

Helpline: 0800 028 28 22
Tel: +44 (0) 1691 680 635
E-mail: info@murray-foundation.org.uk
Web Address: www.murray-foundation.org.uk

Osteosarcoma: Osteosarcoma is the most common type of bone cancer, and the sixth most common type of cancer in children. Although other types of cancer can eventually spread to parts of the skeleton, osteosarcoma is one of the few that actually begin in bones and sometimes spread (or metastasize) elsewhere.

Because osteosarcoma usually develops from osteoblasts (the cells that make growing bone), it most commonly affects teens who are experiencing a growth spurt. Boys are more likely to have osteosarcoma than girls, and most cases of osteosarcoma involve the knee.

Most osteosarcomas arise from random and unpredictable errors in the DNA of growing bone cells during times of intense bone growth. There currently isn't an effective way to prevent this type of cancer. But with the proper diagnosis and treatment, most kids with osteosarcoma do recover.

PPAM Aid: (pneumatic post amputation mobility aid) Early walking aid that often gives new amputees their first taste both of how a prosthetic limb is going to feel pressure wise and of walking upright again. Its simplistic design is highly effective. It consists of a solid metal pylon and an inflatable 'leg' that is placed around the stump then inflated until it fills the pylon, allowing the amputee to walk for a limited time. Not suitable for long-term use.

Paralympics: In 1948, Sir Ludwig Guttmann organized a sports competition involving World War II veterans with a spinal cord injury in Stoke Mandeville, England. Four years later, competitors from the Netherlands joined the games and an international movement was born. Olympic style games for athletes with a disability were organized for the first time in Rome in 1960, now called Paralympics. In Toronto in 1976, other disability groups were added and the idea of merging together different disability groups for international sport competitions was born. In the same year, the first Paralympic Winter Games took place in Sweden.

Today, the Paralympics are elite sport events for athletes from six different disability groups. They emphasize, however, the participants' athletic achievements rather than their disability. The movement has grown dramatically since its first days. The number of athletes participating in Summer Paralympic Games has increased from 400 athletes from 23 countries in Rome in 1960 to 3806 athletes from 136 countries in Athens in 2004.

The Paralympic Games have always been held in the same year as the Olympic Games. Since the Seoul 1988 Paralympic Games and the Albertville 1992 Winter Paralympic Games they have also taken place at the same venues as the Olympics. On 19 June 2001, an agreement was signed between IOC and IPC securing this practice for the future. From the 2012 bid process onwards, the host city chosen to host the Olympic Games will be obliged to also host the Paralympics.

125

Person centred counselling: Person Centred Counselling was developed by Carl Rogers who believed that the individual was a competent architect of his own destiny, was innately able to deal with whatever he experienced and possessed the ability to heal himself. This belief in the strength and integrity of human beings is fundamental to person centred counselling.

The emphasis of person centred counselling is placed upon the relationship between the counsellor and client and on the changes that may take place within the client when the counsellor creates a climate of empathy, genuineness and acceptance.

Phantom limb pain: The cause of phantom pain is not fully understood. It is important to emphasize that the pain is not imagined, and is not the result of a psychological or emotional disturbance. We have learned that the central nervous system (the brain and the spinal cord) is capable of creating "memories" of pain that can cause the pain to persist. Furthermore, normal sensation plays an important role in inhibiting pain. (Notice our tendency to rub an area that has been injured.) The loss of a limb means that pain sensations can persist without the brakes of the normal sensations of touch and movement. Most amputees experience phantom pain at some stage.

Pneumatic knee: A pneumatic cylinder is installed in the knee that uses principles of fluid mechanics to vary the resistance of the knee as the user changes their walking speed. This allows the individual to walk at different cadences and have the prosthetic knee keep pace to ensure the prosthesis is always in the correct position for safety when placing weight onto the prosthesis at heel contact. Pneumatic knee units are usually lighter in weight and less heavy duty than hydraulic knees.

Prosthesis: In medicine, prosthesis is an artificial extension that replaces a missing body part. Prostheses are typically used to replace parts lost by injury (traumatic) or missing from birth (congenital) or to supplement defective body parts.

Prosthetic arm: Prosthetic arms attempt to carry out the some of the roles of the physiological arm like complex manipulation of objects.

Push pull brake/accelerator: The combined push-pull brake and accelerator lever is one of a range of hand control adaptations that are available when a person is unable to use their feet to operate the standard pedals. The lever is usually positioned behind and to the right of the steering wheel, connected by rods/cables to the accelerator and brake pedals and operated by the right hand. In certain circumstances the lever can be fitted to the left of the wheel for left hand operation. This lever is pulled to accelerate and pushed away to brake. A switch or switches may be incorporated onto the lever and conveniently positioned to allow the fingers/thumb of the right hand to operate indicators, horn, lights etc.

This adaptation can be fitted to most vehicles but the system is designed primarily for a vehicle with automatic transmission and for a person who is unable to use or has difficulty using their legs to operate the pedals for accelerating and braking. It is strongly recommended that these controls are fitted to a vehicle with power assisted steering.

Radiotherapy: Radiotherapy is the use of x-rays and similar rays (such as electrons) to treat disease.

Since the discovery of x-rays over one hundred years ago, radiation has been used more and more in medicine, both to help with diagnosis (by taking pictures with x-rays), and as a treatment (radiotherapy). While radiation obviously has to be used very carefully, doctors and radiographers have a lot of experience in its use in medicine.

Many people with cancer will have radiotherapy as part of their treatment. This can be given either as external radiotherapy from outside the body using x-rays or from within the body as internal radiotherapy.

Radiotherapy works by destroying the cancer cells in the treated area. Although normal cells are also sometimes damaged by the radiotherapy, they can repair themselves.

Radiotherapy treatment can cure some cancers and can reduce the chance of a cancer coming back after surgery. It may be used to reduce cancer symptoms.

Some people find that the side effects are very mild and that they just feel tired during their course of radiotherapy.

Residual arm/ leg: portion of the limb that remains after amputation. Also known more commonly as a 'stump'.

Septicaemia: Septicaemia is a bacterial infection of the blood, commonly known as blood poisoning.

Often it's a complication of another infection, such as of the lungs or kidneys, and occurs when the bacteria escape that part of the body and get into the bloodstream.

This bacteria can also come from burns, infected wounds, boils and tooth abscesses

The symptoms of septicaemia develop rapidly and may include:
- High fever
- Violent shivering
- Faintness
- Cold and pale hands and feet
- Rapid and shallow breathing
- Restlessness
- Delirium
- Shock
- Loss of consciousness

When infection is with meningocuccus bacteria, a rash may appear. This starts off as small red-purple spots that grow quickly to become blotchy and look like little bruises. It doesn't fade when pressed.

Silicon liner: More expensive type of prosthesis liner that is more suitable for patients with skin grafts or sensitive skin. Long term use can actually reduce the appearance of scars.

Skin graft: A skin graft is when you skin is taken from one area of the body and attached to another area where no skin exists. It might be necessary for extensive wounds or extensive burns; or a surgical procedure requiring skin grafts for healing to occur.

Steering ball: Similar to the part on the wheel of a forklift truck. These devices clamp to the wheel and are designed to aid one handed steering. Two versions are available, one is designed to remain on the wheel and the other can be quickly released on the driver's preference.

Suction socket: A stump-receiving socket for an artificial limb which has an elastic diaphragm that sealingly engages a patient's stump when the stump is fully received in the socket.

Transfer/transferring The technique used to transfer from a wheelchair to the WC and back varies according to factors such as: the size and design of the wheelchair; the level of function that the disabled person has (for example, strength in upper limbs); whether the transfer is independent or assisted; and personal preference.

This may be done with the wheelchair in any of the transfer positions mentioned above. Assistance is needed when the wheelchair user has little or no functional use of the lower limbs and impaired upper limbs. He/she will need to be manually lifted or heaved from the wheelchair seat to the WC seat and back. Clear, unobstructed space on both sides of the WC is important to allow the assistant (or assistants) to bend, turn and move freely when lifting a disabled person's weight if they are unable to transfer themselves.

Trauma: In the context of this book, this refers to injuries caused by an accident or assault requiring immediate medical attention, as opposed to having surgery on an elective basis (when you know it's going to happen).

Wet floor shower room: Wet floor shower areas are increasingly popular as an alternative to fitting a shower tray, providing completely open and level access. They are ideal for wheelchair users, and a good choice where it is not practical to install a tray.

A number of companies now produce wet floor formers, with an inbuilt gradient to assist drainage. These are laid level with the existing floor and then the whole area can be covered with a non-slip vinyl, to give a waterproof surface without any lips or ramps.

Specially designed doors and screens, which can be fitted directly to a wet floor, make an enclosure to suit the space and the user's needs. Most council housing providers can provide this facility.

Wheelchair (Electric): Electric wheelchairs are usually a lot heavier than manual wheelchairs because the frame has to be stronger in order to support the battery and motors. The level of sophistication in electric wheelchairs also varies widely, from just using standard batteries and a joy stick controller, right up to using microprocessor controlled gyroscopic circuitry which enables the chair to rise on two wheels!

When choosing an electric wheelchair, be sure to use a reputable make from a licence supplier. This will ensure you receive full back up if the chair needs servicing. Also beware of second hand electric wheelchairs, as they can suffer from cracked frames, faulty batteries and worn out motors.

The way that Electric wheelchairs are propelled also varies, and these different methods give different characteristics to the wheelchairs. The following are the three basic methods of propulsion:
- Rear Wheel Drive Wheelchairs-
- This is the most common method of drive for an electric wheelchair. This method makes the wheelchair fast, but can give a poor turning capability when compared to front and mid wheel drive chairs.

- Mid Wheel Drive Wheelchairs-
- This method of drive gives the best turning capability of all the wheelchairs. The wheelchair can be a little unsteady when

130

starting and stopping though, and may not be suitable for uneven surfaces.

- Front Wheel Drive Wheelchairs-
- This method of drive gives a lower top speed than rear wheel drive chairs, but offers a good turning capability.

Wheelchair (Manual): If you have the ability to push your wheelchair, you will need what is known as a manual wheelchair. These wheelchairs are propelled by the user by pushing rims on the back wheels.

There are many materials a wheelchair can be made from which include:

- Steel
- Aluminium
- Titanium
- Carbon Fibre

There are two types of wheelchair which to consider. These are a rigid frame wheelchair and a folding frame wheelchair

Generally, a rigid frame wheelchair will consist of a welded frame on which the person sits. The back of the chair has the ability to fold down, and the wheels have a quick release mechanism to enable easy transportation and storage of the wheelchair.

Most rigid frame wheelchairs are made from either aluminium or titanium, but there are some specialist wheelchairs made from carbon fibre. A lightweight rigid frame wheelchair can weigh as little as 10lbs without its wheels. As the chair is lighter, it will be easier to push, therefore putting less stress on your shoulder joints.

As rigid frame wheelchairs have less moving parts, they are generally stronger than folding wheelchairs and last longer.

A folding frame wheelchair is a wheelchair whose frame is collapsible sideways by the use of an X mechanism in the frame. This mechanism is lockable, and the wheelchair folds on release of two locking levers on the chair.

Because the folding wheelchair has an X mechanism, locking levers and re-enforcing struts, it is usually more heavy than a rigid frame wheelchair. Folding wheelchairs also have movable footrests which allow the chair to collapse. Early folding chairs were made from steel, but now days they are made from aluminium or titanium.

As there are more moving parts in the folding chair, and movable joints, the chair is not as durable as a rigid frame wheelchair. This in turn will mean a higher maintenance is required to keep the wheelchair in good condition.

6107787R00078

Printed in Great Britain
by Amazon.co.uk, Ltd.,
Marston Gate.